青年学者文丛

SSCI 期刊学术论文写作指南

葛子刚　编著

北京邮电大学出版社
www.buptpress.com

内容简介

本书介绍和剖析了SSCI检索期刊所发论文的结构和写作要点，并对SSCI期刊的检索、投稿等环节做了详细介绍。全书共分为3章，第1章介绍了如何在SSCI检索库中获取自己投稿的目标期刊，并介绍了SSCI期刊对于投稿的要求；第2章是本书的主要部分，从论文写作的结构入手，逐一介绍了论文标题、关键词、引言、文献回顾、研究问题、研究方法、研究结果、讨论部分和结论部分的写作方法，并介绍了一些常用的表达方式和参考文献的获取与使用；第3章介绍了投稿过程中需要注意的事项，尤其是用实例详细解释了大修和小修的应对套路。

本书适合有学术写作需求的高校人文社科类教师、研究生等群体使用。

图书在版编目(CIP)数据

SSCI期刊学术论文写作指南 / 葛子刚编著. -- 北京：北京邮电大学出版社，2021.8 (2024.10重印)

ISBN 978-7-5635-6362-3

Ⅰ. ①S… Ⅱ. ①葛… Ⅲ. ①论文—写作—指南 Ⅳ. ①H152.3-62

中国版本图书馆CIP数据核字(2021)第069682号

策划编辑：姚　顺　刘纳新　　责任编辑：廖　娟　　封面设计：七星博纳

出版发行：北京邮电大学出版社
社　　址：北京市海淀区西土城路10号
邮政编码：100876
发 行 部：电话：010-62282185　传真：010-62283578
E-mail：publish@bupt.edu.cn
经　　销：各地新华书店
印　　刷：河北虎彩印刷有限公司
开　　本：720 mm×1 000 mm　1/16
印　　张：10.5
字　　数：210千字
版　　次：2021年8月第1版
印　　次：2024年10月第9次印刷

ISBN 978-7-5635-6362-3　　　　　　　　　　　　　　　定价：32.00元

· 如有印装质量问题，请与北京邮电大学出版社发行部联系 ·

前　言

如今，国内科研人员越来越注重国际交流，而将研究成果发表在国际高水平期刊无疑是宣传、交流科研成果的有效方式之一。高校等学术研究机构也越来越以在高水平国际期刊发表论文作为对科研人员进行考核的一项标准。自然学科领域的期刊众多，SCI 检索的期刊也是多如牛毛，而与之相对的人文社科领域，SSCI 检索的期刊数目却相对较少，发表难度也较大。在 SSCI 检索的期刊上发表论文对于国内人文社科领域的投稿人来说有两大难点：一是语言，因为这些期刊基本都是以英语为写作语言，对英语表达水平要求较高；二是很多人对这些期刊的论文写作结构和投稿流程不是很清楚。国内专论此方面的书籍很少，抑或是过于专业化，对于初涉 SSCI 期刊投稿的学者来说不易理解和掌握。鉴于此，本书力图以浅显易懂的语言对 SSCI 检索期刊的投稿、写作等各环节做详细解读，以飨读者。

首先，在内容选择上，本书尽量考虑得周详。内容覆盖了期刊选择、论文章节写作以及投稿过程中大修小修的应对等环节，因为这每一个环节对于初涉国际期刊的投稿人来说都是及其重要的。其次，在语言上尽量做到平实易懂，避免晦涩的语言表达方式，在剖析问题时结合了大量的实例，而且对于实例又做了精细的解读，这样安排的目的就在于避免读者在有疑惑的地方感到无助。

本书内容是按照期刊选择、论文写作到投稿这三大环节安排下来的，而每一个环节又被细分为众多的小环节。书中每一小节都针对某一特定内容展开，开头就直奔主题，给出解决方案，接着列举大量实例，最后给出该实例的解析。

本书的写作语言浅显易懂，故可以作为高校和科研机构研究生的学术写作课程的教材。作为教材使用时,教师可以专注于第 2 章内容的讲解,对于第 1 章和第 3 章则稍加解读即可。

  虽然作者有多年的学术论文写作经验,并已在 SSCI 期刊发表多篇学术论文,但是在此书的写作上难免有纰漏与错误,欢迎广大读者批评指正,不胜感激。

葛子刚

目 录

第 1 章　SSCI 检索简介 ·· 1

1.1　SSCI 期刊名录的获取与筛选 ·· 1

1.2　SSCI 期刊的发表目标与范围 ·· 4

1.3　SSCI 期刊的投稿系统 ·· 5

1.4　SSCI 期刊投稿的具体要求 ·· 7

第 2 章　SSCI 论文的结构与写作 ··· 8

2.1　SSCI 论文的基本结构 ·· 8

2.2　SSCI 论文的标题和关键词 ·· 9

　　2.2.1　标题 ·· 9

　　2.2.2　关键词 ·· 13

2.3　摘要 ·· 15

2.4　引言 ·· 17

2.5　文献回顾 ··· 22

2.6　研究问题 ··· 32

2.7　研究方法 ··· 37

2.8　研究结果 ··· 47

2.9 讨论 ·· 53

2.10 结论 ·· 60

2.11 SSCI 论文整体解析实例 ·· 63

2.12 SSCI 论文常用表达方式 ··· 105

2.13 SSCI 论文参考文献的获取与使用 ································· 108

第 3 章 从投稿到发表 ·· 113

3.1 稿件状态 ·· 113

3.2 大修和小修的应对 ·· 114

3.3 大修应对实例 ··· 118

3.4 接收后事项 ·· 152

参考文献 ·· 155

第1章 SSCI 检索简介

SSCI 全称为 Social Sciences Citation Index(社会科学引文索引),最初是由美国科学信息研究所(Institute for Scientific Information,ISI)创建的。2016 年,运营 SSCI 和 SCI 业务的汤森路透(Thomson Reuters)将 SSCI 和 SCI 业务出售给了 Onex 公司和霸菱亚洲(Baring Private Equity Asia),并成立了新的运营公司 Clarivate Analytics。

SSCI 和 SCI 定位不同,SCI 收录的期刊是科技类,而 SSCI 收录的期刊则是人文社科类,包括法律、经济、历史、教育、心理等学科期刊。每年,SSCI 都会对其收录的期刊进行评估和筛选,会新收录一批,也会剔除一批。

1.1 SSCI 期刊名录的获取与筛选

对于 SSCI 收录的期刊名单,我们可以在其运营公司(Clarivate Analytics)的网站上免费获取。该网址目前为 https://mjl.clarivate.com/collection-list-downloads,打开该网址后,可以看到如图 1-1 所示的页面。

这个页面提供了几大核心期刊库的期刊目录下载链接,包括 SCIE、SSCI、AHCI 和 ESCI,点击图标即可下载这些核心库里的期刊表了。下载下来的期刊表是一个 EXCEL 文件,文件里用列表形式给出了期刊的名称、ISSN(期刊号)、eISSN(在线期刊号)、出版商和出版地址。

此外,我们还可以在以下页面进行具体期刊的搜索:https://mjl.clarivate.com/search-results。我们可以在页面的搜索框里输入期刊的 ISSN 或标题词进行搜索,同时可以在页面左侧的核心库中进行核心库的选择(SCIE/SSCI/AHCI/ESCI)。具体期刊搜索页面如图 1-2 所示。

在图 1-2 所示的页面里,左侧导航栏还可以选择期刊所属的类别(Category),如图 1-3 所示。

Web of Science Core Collection

Last Updated: December 18, 2019

The *Web of Science Core Collection* includes the *Science Citation Index Expanded (SCIE), Social Sciences Citation Index (SSCI), Arts & Humaniti Sources Citation Index (ESCI)*. *Web of Science Core Collection* includes only journals that demonstrate high levels of editorial rigor and best

Each collection list download includes the journal title, ISSN/eISSN, publisher name and address.

Science Citation Index Expanded (SCIE)   Social Sciences Citation Index (SSCI)   Arts & Humanities Citation Index (AHCI)   Emerging Sources Citation Index (ESCI)

图 1-1　SSCI 期刊获取页面

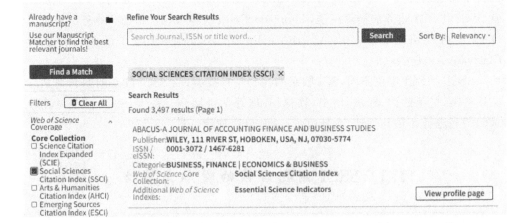

图 1-2　具体期刊搜索页面

图 1-3　期刊类别

在类别（Category）下的搜索框内可以输入期刊所属的分类，如 Education、Psychology 等。

在获取了相关类别的期刊目录后，我们需要对文章可投的期刊做一定的筛选。筛选一般需要考虑以下问题：1）论文的主题和期刊主题的契合度；2）期刊的录用难度。这里我们以 SSCI 教育类期刊为例，此类期刊涵盖了教育的各个方面，如教育技术、教师教育、教学类、语言教学类、教育心理类、教育理论类等。首先，我们需要根据自己论文的主题来搜索相应的可以投稿的期刊。其次，我们还要考虑期刊的录用难度。录用难度可以结合期刊的出刊频率和期刊当年的影响因子来判断，如何获取这些信息呢？方法如下：首先在图 1-2 所示的搜索框内输入想查找的期刊题名或者 ISSN，然后页面就会出现搜索结果。在出现的结果中，点击期刊后面的"View profile page"可看到该期刊出刊频率、出版语言、出版地等基本信息。

图 1-4 显示了 *Advances in Health Sciences Education* 这份期刊的基本情况，

图 1-4　期刊的出刊频率

包括刊名、出刊频率、刊号、被收录的检索库、出版商等。可以看出,这份期刊的出刊频率是双月(bimonthly),刊号是 1382-4996,出版商是 Springer,被收录的检索库有 SSCI、SCIE 等,2018 年该期刊的影响因子是 2.761。此外,期刊的常见出刊频率还包括月刊(monthly)、季刊(quarterly)、一年三期(triannual)等。一般来说,月刊或双月刊由于每年出版的频率较高,可以接收的文章数量也相对高于季刊等。

此外,图 1-4 所示的页面上有三处"Visit Site"字样,分别在"Journal Website"旁边、"Publisher Website"旁边和"Submission Website"旁边,点击这三处的"Visit Site",我们可以分别访问该期刊的页面、出版商的主页和该期刊投稿的页面。在期刊的主页上,我们可以查看该刊物每期大约刊登的论文数量,这也有助于判断论文被该刊物接受的难度。除此之处,刊物的出版频率、刊号、检索源、出版商、影响因子等信息也可以在期刊的主页上看到。例如,图 1-5 列出了 *Interactive Learning Environments* 这份期刊在 2018 年的影响因子为 1.929,虽然该期刊每年出刊 8 次,但是由于影响因子将近 2,所以中稿的竞争还是挺激烈的。

图 1-5 期刊主页给出的信息

此外,由于 SSCI 对于收录的期刊会进行不定时评估,所以会发生"新收录"(newly added)或"被剔除"(dropped)的现象,特别是那些影响因子非常小的期刊可能会被剔除。所以,我们在投稿前最好用以上方法进行查看。一般来说,期刊会在主页上写明自己被哪些数据库所收录。

1.2 SSCI 期刊的发表目标与范围

同类别的期刊,在其具体定位上也可能会不同,这就要求我们在投稿前明确期刊的目标与范围。有两种方法可以让我们明确期刊的目标与范围,一是浏览该期刊已经刊发论文的题目，二是查看期刊主页上写明的"Aims and Scope"（目标与范围）①。图1-6显示了 Innovations in Education and Teaching International 这份期刊的发表范围。该期刊明确表示接受的文章主题是高等教育或继续教育领域，论文需要强调研究、经历、学术和评价，而不接受只对实践方法进行描述的论文。

图1-6 期刊的发表范围

除了查看期刊明确标明的发表范围，我们还可以浏览该期刊已经刊发论文的题目。一般来说，浏览论文的题目就可以判断该期刊喜欢刊发哪类文章。再以 Innovations in Education and Teaching International 这份期刊为例，其2018年第1期刊登的论文是：1) To what extent does "flipping" make lessons effective in a multimedia production class? 2) Peer e-tutoring: Effects on students' participation and interaction style in online courses; 3) The role of knowledge sharing in enhancing innovation: a comparative study of public and private higher education institutions in Iraq; 4) Learning by identification of mistakes in workings in engineering modules; 5) A comparison between the effectiveness of PBL and LBL on improving problem-solving abilities of medical students using questioning 等。浏览这些文章的题目，我们发现这些文章都和教学创新有关，所以教学类文章被此刊接收的可能性较大。

1.3 SSCI 期刊的投稿系统

目前，SSCI 期刊普遍合作的投稿系统主要有 ScholarOne Manuscripts、Evise 和 Elsevier Editorial System。这些投稿系统大同小异，虽然界面不同，但是投稿流程基本一致。图1-7、图1-8和图1-9分别展示了这三种投稿系统的界面（分别为三种期刊使用，Computers & Education 使用 Elsevier Editorial System，Technology, Pedagogy

---

① Elsevier 等出版商出版的期刊并没有用"Aims and Scope"进行标明，但是在期刊主页上都会有相关说明。

and Education 使用 ScholarOne Manuscripts，*The Internet and Higher Education* 使用 Evise)。

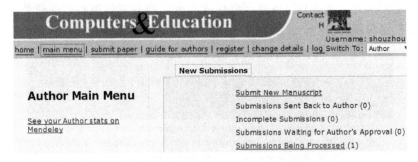

图 1-7 Elsevier Editorial System 投稿系统界面

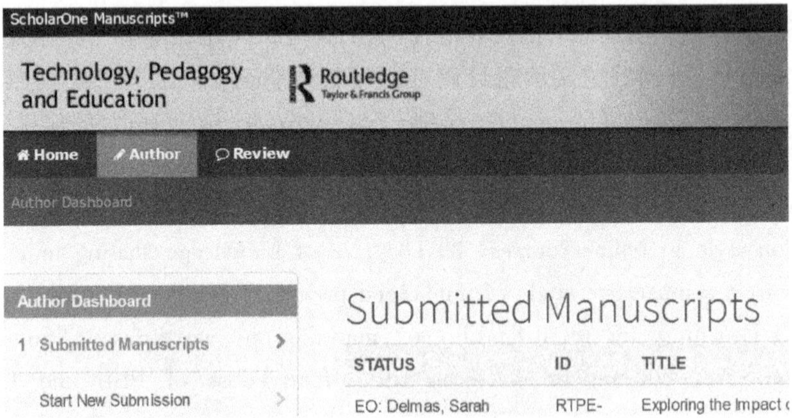

图 1-8 ScholarOne Manuscripts 投稿系统界面

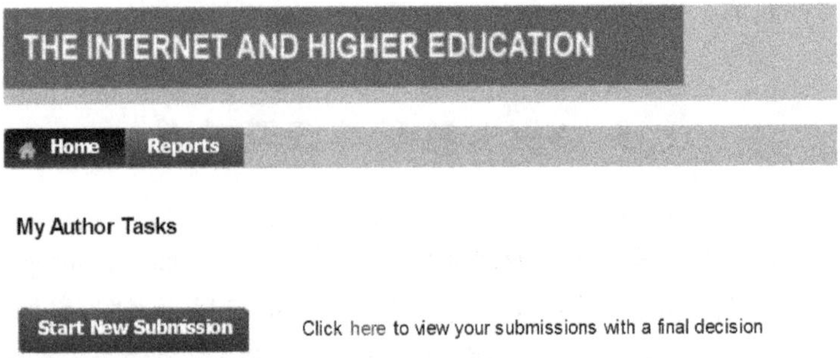

图 1-9 Evise 投稿系统界面

在这三种投稿系统里，如果我们要新投稿，则只需要点击各界面里的"Start New Submission"或"Submit New Manuscript"即可。

需要指出的是,目前多数期刊都要求作者在标题页(Title Page)标注并在投稿系统里关联自己的科研人员和投稿身份识别码(ORCID),这个识别码其实就相当于一个国际通用的科研身份证明,可以在 https://orcid.org/注册获得。

1.4 SSCI 期刊投稿的具体要求

投稿前,作者需要按照期刊的具体要求对论文的格式等方面做出修改,否则即使在投稿系统提交,等来的也是"返回作者"(Returned to Author),让修改后再投,这无疑大大耽误稿件的后续工作。期刊主页上一般都会专门列出投稿指南(Guide for Authors 或 Instructions for Authors),我们需要认真阅读这些说明,按照说明准备材料。我们需要关注以下一些要求:1)字号的要求;2)图表是直接嵌入文章,还是需要单独放在另一页;3)除了匿名版论文稿件之外,需不需要提供非匿名版本;4)标题页(Title Page)包括的信息;5)需不需要写投稿信(Cover Letter);6)需不需要列出论文的关键创新点(Highlights);7)关键词是自拟,还是需要从给出的词语中选取;8)是否需要在标题页对"利益冲突"(Conflicts of Interest)进行申明等。图 1-10 所示为 Computers & Education 期刊主页上的"作者指南",可以看出,期刊对投稿过程中的各个环节都做了说明。

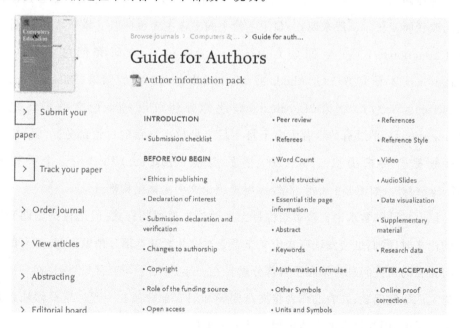

图 1-10　期刊主页上的"作者指南"

第2章 SSCI论文的结构与写作

本章将对论文各部分的写作要点做详细介绍,掌握这些写作要点可以提高论文在SSCI期刊投稿的中稿率。

2.1 SSCI论文的基本结构

各种期刊对于学术论文基本结构的要求大体上是一致的,并不会随着投稿期刊的改变而变化。一般来说,一篇学术论文的主体主要包括以下部分:1)引言部分(Introduction);2)文献回顾(Literature Review);3)研究问题(Research Questions);4)研究方法(Methods或Methodology);5)研究结果(Results);6)讨论(Discussion);7)结论(Conclusions,此部分还可以列出论文的不足之处(Limitations),不过有的学者倾向于将不足之处放在文章的讨论部分)。此外,期刊一般都会要求提供150～200字的摘要(Abstract)和3～5个关键词(Keywords)。如图2-1所示,框线标出了该论文的主体结构部分。

以上提到的学术论文基本结构是大多数论文遵循的样式,但是在浏览期刊发表的论文时,我们也会发现有些论文作者会对这几大基本部分稍做改变,如有的作者将论文的研究问题直接和引言部分融合在一起,介绍了研究背景后,直接列出当前论文的研究问题;还有的作者将文献回顾和引言部分放在一起。这些做法都是可以接受的,因为论文的大体框架还是上述那些。

第 2 章　SSCI 论文的结构与写作

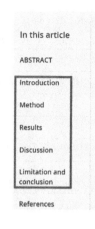

图 2-1　论文的主体结构

2.2　SSCI 论文的标题和关键词

2.2.1　标题

如果学术论文的标题起得好,会给编辑留下非常好的第一印象,从而使论文得以顺利送审(Send for Review)。当然,标题必须是和内容紧密相关并能高度概括内容的,而不是为了吸引眼球,却和内容风马牛不相及的。总的说来,SSCI 期刊的论文标题需要遵循以下规则:1)期刊对标题字数的要求;2)标题的整体结构一般是名词性短语(动名词短语也可),有时也可以用问句甚至祈使句作为标题。下面以 SSCI 期刊 *Computers & Education* 2018 年 6 月刊发的论文标题为例来说明。该期刊这一期共发表了 12 篇论文,我们来看看它们的标题。

1) 论文 1 (Tsay, Kofinas, & Luo, 2018)

标题:Enhancing student learning experience with technology-mediated gamification: An empirical study

标题分析:此标题用了动名词短语(Enhancing…),大意为"利用基于技术的游戏来提高学生的学习体验:一项实证研究"。

2) 论文 2 (Tsai, Lin, Hong, & Tai, 2018)

标题:The effects of metacognition on online learning interest and continuance to learn with MOOCs

标题分析:这个标题用了名词短语(The effects…),大意为"元认知对网络学习兴趣和利用慕课进行学习持续性的影响"。

3）论文 3（Bano，Zowghi，Kearney，Schuck，& Aubusson，2018）

标题：Mobile learning for science and mathematics school education：A systematic review of empirical evidence

标题分析：这个标题用了名词短语（Mobile learning…），大意为"移动学习在科学与数学学校教育中的应用：实证研究的系统综述"。

4）论文 4（Al-Rahmi，Alias，Othman，Marin，& Tur，2018）

标题：A model of factors affecting learning performance through the use of social media in Malaysian higher education

标题分析：此标题用了名词短语（A model…），大意为"马来西亚高等教育中使用社交媒体影响学习成绩的因素模型"。

5）论文 5（Hsu & Wang，2018）

标题：Applying game mechanics and student-generated questions to an online puzzle-based game learning system to promote algorithmic thinking skills

标题分析：这个标题用了动名词短语（Applying…），大意为"将游戏机制和学生生成的问题应用于一个在线解密游戏学习系统，以提高算术思维能力"。

6）论文 6（Barak & Asakle，2018）

标题：AugmentedWorld：Facilitating the creation of location-based questions

标题分析：这个标题是名词（AugmentedWorld）＋动名词（Facilitating…）的格式，大意为"增强世界：促进基于位置的问题的创建"。

7）论文 7（Förster，Weiser，& Maur，2018）

标题：How feedback provided by voluntary electronic quizzes affects learning outcomes of university students in large classes

标题分析：本标题是一个问句（How…），大意为"自愿电子测验提供的反馈对大班大学生学习成绩的影响"，也可以翻译成原本的问句形式："自愿电子测验提供的反馈是如何对大班大学生的学习成绩产生影响的呢？"

8）论文 8（Barak，2018）

标题：Are digital natives open to change? Examining flexible thinking and resistance to change

标题分析：本标题由一个问句（Are…?）和一个动名词短语（Examining…）构成，大意为"数码原住民是否愿意改变？审视柔性思维与变革阻力"。

9）论文 9（Vega-Hernández，Patino-Alonso，& Galindo-Villardón，2018）

标题：Multivariate characterization of university students using the ICT for learning

标题分析：本标题是由一个名词性短语（Multivariate characterization…）构成，大意为"大学生使用 ICT 进行学习的多元特征分析"。

10) 论文 10（Wang，Zhang，Du，& Wang，2018）

标题：Development and measurement validity of an instrument for the impact of technology-mediated learning on learning processes

标题分析：本标题是一个名词短语（Development and measurement validity…），大意为"一个测量以技术为中介的学习对学习过程影响的工具的开发及其测量效度"。

11) 论文 11（Choi，Cristol，& Gimbert，2018）

标题：Teachers as digital citizens：The influence of individual backgrounds, internet use and psychological characteristics on teachers' levels of digital citizenship

标题分析：此标题是名词短语（Teachers…）＋名词短语（The influence…）构成，大意为"教师作为数字公民：个人背景、网络使用和心理特征对教师数字化公民水平的影响"。

12) 论文 12（Claro et al.，2018）

标题：Teaching in a Digital Environment（TIDE）：Defining and measuring teachers' capacity to develop students' digital information and communication skills

标题分析：本标题是由名词短语（Teaching…）＋动名词短语（Defining and measuring…）构成，大意为"数字环境下的教学：界定和衡量教师培养学生数字信息和交流技能的能力"。

可以看出，在这一期的 12 篇论文中，有 10 篇论文的标题是由名词或动名词或两种皆有的形式构成，另外 2 篇论文的标题则是由问句或问句搭配动名词短语的形式构成。

我们再来看看管理类顶级 SSCI 期刊 *Academy of Management Review* 在 2019 年第 2 期发表的文章类论文，论文题目如下。

1) 论文 1（Glynn，2019）

标题：2018 presidential address—the mission of community and the promise of collective action

标题分析：本标题是由一个简单的名词短语加上破折号后面的同位语成分组成，大意为"2018 年总统演讲——社区的使命和集体行动的承诺"。

2) 论文 2（Parker，krause，& Devers，2019）

标题：How firm reputation shapes managerial discretion

标题分析：这个标题采用疑问句的形式，大意为"企业声誉如何塑造管理判断力？"。

3) 论文 3（Fisher，2019）

标题：Online communities and firm advantages

标题分析:这个标题是由两个名词短语用 and 这个并列连词连接而成,大意为"网络社区和企业优势"。

4) 论文 4 (Durand, Hawn, & Ioannou, 2019)

标题:Willing and able: a general model of organizational responses to normative pressures

标题分析:这个标题由两个形容词外加名词短语构成,大意为"意愿和能力:组织应对规范性压力的一般模型"。这里要注意的是,形容词不可以单独用作标题,因为它无法讲述研究的主题到底是什么,所以用了形容词后,一般都需要另外用名词短语等进行进一步的解释。只有这样,读者才能明白标题到底讲述的是什么研究内容。此外,在翻译成中文时,也可以将形容词名词化,如本标题中的 willing(愿意的)和 able(有能力的)这两个形容词被翻译成了"意愿和能力"。

5) 论文 5 (Weik, 2019)

标题:Understanding institutional endurance: The role of dynamic form, harmony, and rhythm in institutions

标题分析:这个标题的主体是一个动名词短语,冒号后面的名词短语则进一步补充了研究的具体内容,大意为"理解制度耐力:动态形式、和谐与韵律在制度中的作用"。

6) 论文 6 (Waege & Weber, 2019)

标题:Institutional complexity and organizational change: An open polity perspective

标题分析:本标题由两个名词短语构成,中间用了并列连词 and 连接,冒号后面又是一个名词性短语进一步补充说明论文采用的视角,大意为"制度复杂性与组织变革:一个开放的政治视角"。

7) 论文 7 (Li, McAllister, Ilies, & Gloor, 2019)

标题:Schadenfreude: A counternormative observer response to workplace mistreatment

标题分析:这个标题的主体是一个名词 shadenfreude,冒号后面是一个名词性短语"A counternormative observer response"加一个介宾成分"to workplace mistreatment"来说明研究的内容,标题大意为"幸灾乐祸:旁观者对工作场所不公平待遇的反规范反应"。

8) 论文 8 (Gill, 2019)

标题:The significance of suffering in organizations: Understanding variation in workers' responses to multiple modes of control

标题分析:这个标题的主体是一个名词短语,冒号后面用了动名词短语,大意为"组织中痛苦的意义:理解工人对多种控制模式的反应的差异"。

9) 论文 9 (Kudesia, 2019)

标题:Mindfulness as metacognitive practice

标题分析：此标题的主体就是一个名词 mindfulness（正念），后面用 as 引导了一个名词短语来说明"正念"的作用，这也是论文要讨论的话题，就是把正念当作一种元认知实践的方法。本标题大意为"把正念当作元认知实践"。

10) 论文 10（Puranik，Koopman，Vough，& Gamache，2019）

标题：They want what I've got (I think)：The causes and consequences of attributing coworker behavior to envy

标题分析：本标题主体是一个陈述句，冒号后面用了名词短语进一步说明本文的研究内容。大意为"我之所有，他之觊觎：将同事行为归于嫉妒的因和果"。

和教育类论文一样，以上这些管理类论文的标题也多为名词或动名词，即使是疑问句或陈述句，也多用名词短语或动名词短语进行补充说明。

2.2.2 关键词

关键词的选取有两种情况，一种是期刊规定要从指定的关键词词库中选取，另一种是自拟。前一种关键词，只需要在投稿时按照期刊提供的关键词词库并对照论文的主题进行挑选即可，如 SSCI 期刊 *Computers & Education* 就要求作者从其提供的关键词中进行挑选。如果向这本期刊投稿时没有注意到这一点，那么在格式审查（Technical Check）时就不会被通过。图 2-2 所示就是 *Computers & Education* 投稿系统提供的关键词选择范围。

Keywords

Immediately after the abstract, provide a maximum of **5 keywords**. These keywords will be used for indexing purposes and should be chosen from the following list: *adult learning; applications in subject areas; architectures for educational technology system; authoring tools and methods; computer-mediated communication; cooperative/collaborative learning; country-specific developments; cross-cultural projects; distance education and telelearning; distributed learning environments; elementary education; evaluation methodologies; evaluation of CAL systems; gender studies; human-computer interface; improving classroom teaching; intelligent tutoring systems; interactive learning environments; interdisciplinary projects; learning communities; lifelong learning; media in education; multimedia/hypermedia systems; navigation ; pedagogical issues; post-secondary education; programming and programming languages; public spaces and computing; secondary education; simulations; teaching/learning strategies; virtual reality.*

图 2-2 某期刊的关键词词库

大多数期刊并不限制关键词的选取，所以作者可以自己挑选适合论文主题的关键词。这种情况下，关键词可以根据论文题目和摘要进行挑选。下面以两篇论文的关键词为例。

1) 论文 1 (Sun, Xie, & Anderman, 2018)

标题:The role of **self-regulated learning** in students' success in **flipped** undergraduate math courses

摘要:Based upon the **self-regulated learning** theory, this study examined the relationships between academic achievement and three key self-regulatory constructs - prior domain knowledge, **self-efficacy**, and the use of **learning strategies** - in two **flipped** undergraduate math courses. **Structural equation modeling** was employed as the primary method to analyze the relationships in both the pre-class and in-class learning environments of the **flipped** courses. The results of the study showed that students' **self-efficacy** in learning math and the use of help seeking strategies were all significantly positively related with academic achievement in both pre- and in-class learning environments. In addition, students' **self-efficacy** in collaborative learning had a positive impact on their use of help seeking strategies during in-class learning. The theoretical and instructional implications are discussed.

关键词:Flipped classroom; Self-regulated learning; Self-efficacy; Learning Strategies; Structural equation modeling

备注:论文题目和摘要中的粗体文字与关键词是重合的。

2) 论文 2 (Cordewener, Hasselman, Verhoeven, & Bosman, 2018)

标题:The Role of Instruction for **Spelling Performance** and **Spelling Consciousness**

摘要:This study examined the role of instruction for **spelling performance** and **spelling consciousness** in the Dutch language. **Spelling consciousness** is the ability to reflect on one's spelling and correct errors. A sample of 115 third-grade spellers was assigned to a **strategy-instruction**, **strategic-monitoring**, **self-monitoring**, or control condition representing different types of metacognitive aspects. The results showed that students in all three training conditions made more progress in both **spelling performance** and **spelling consciousness** than students in the control condition. With respect to **spelling consciousness**, only students in the **strategy-instruction** condition made significant improvement between pretest and posttest. Students made more progress in **spelling performance** on regular words than on loan words. Students in all four conditions became more accurate at assessing which words they could spell correctly. Students in the control condition more frequently overestimated their spelling ability.

关键词:Self-monitoring; spelling performance; spelling consciousness; strategy instruction; strategic monitoring

备注:论文题目和摘要中的粗体文字是和关键词重合的。

从以上例子可以看出,论文的关键词基本都来自论文的题目和摘要,这是因为论文的题目和摘要是对论文主题的高度概括,关键词也需要和论文主题保持一致,从而三者得以互相呼应。

2.3 摘　　要

论文的摘要位于正文之前,但其实作者通常是在完成论文正文后才写摘要,因为摘要是对论文的高度概括,没有完成正文,我们很难写出摘要来。SSCI 期刊论文的摘要字数一般要求 150~200 字,所以需要用高度概括的语言描述清楚论文的主题。一篇合格的论文摘要主要包括以下四个方面:1)研究目的;2)研究方法;3)研究结果;4)结论。在摘要中,研究背景可写可不写,具体得看期刊对摘要字数的要求。我们应尽量将摘要的重点放在研究目的、研究方法、研究结果和结论方面。下面我们以两篇已经刊发在 SSCI 期刊上的论文摘要为例进行说明。

摘要 1(Hylton, Levy, & Dringus, 2016)

Deception and dishonesty in online exams are believed to link to their unmonitored nature where users appear to have the opportunity to collaborate or utilize unauthorized resources during these assessments. The primary goal of this study was to investigate the deterrent effect of Webcam-based proctoring on misconduct during online exams. This study involved an experimental design in comparing an experimental group and a control group. Both groups attended the same course, used the same e-learning system, with the same instructor, and took the same set of online exams. One group was monitored by a Web-based proctor while the other was not monitored. The results indicated no statistically significant difference between the scores of the two groups, although the nonproctored group had slightly higher scores. There was a statistically significant difference found on the time taken to complete the online exams where the proctored group used significantly less time to complete their exams. The results of a post-experiment survey indicated that those who were not proctored perceived to have experienced greater levels of opportunity to engage in misconduct than those who were monitored by a Web-based proctor.

摘要分析：

1）第1句属于研究背景介绍，大意为"在线考试中的欺骗和不诚实行为被认为与他们不受监控的性质有关，在这些测试中，用户似乎有机会合作或利用未经授权的资源。"

2）第2句则介绍了论文的研究目标，大意为"本研究的主要目的是研究基于网络摄像头的监考对在线考试中不端行为的震慑作用。"

3）第3、4、5句描述了论文的研究方法，大意为"本研究采用实验设计比较实验组和对照组，两组学生都参加了相同的课程，使用相同的电子学习系统，相同的授课老师，并参加了相同的在线考试。其中一组由网络监考人员监控，而另一组则没有监控。"

4）第6、7句则是研究结果，大意为"结果显示，两组的得分差异无统计学意义，但非监考组的得分稍高。两组在完成在线考试的时间上有统计学上的显著差异，被监考的小组使用的考试时间明显较少。"

5）第8句是研究结论，大意是"实验后的调查结果表明，那些没有被监考的学生比受到网络监考的学生有更大的机会在考试中发生不端行为。"

摘要 2（Ge，2015）

This study aims to investigate the effectiveness of a storytelling approach in Chinese adult e-learners' vocabulary learning. Two classes of 60 students participated in the experiment, with 30 in the experimental group and 30 in the control group. The storytelling approach and the rote memorization approach were employed by the two groups respectively in one teaching session of 30 minutes. Two post-tests were administered to the two groups, with one completed immediately after the teaching and the other assigned three weeks later. A questionnaire survey was also assigned to the experimental group to obtain the learners' perceptions of the storytelling approach. The results of the data analysis showed that the storytelling method was more effective than rote memorization in both short-term retention and long-term retention, though its effects tended to diminish a little bit with time. Possible suggestions to perfect the method were given in the paper.

摘要分析：

1）第1句描述了论文的研究目的，大意为"本研究旨在探讨在中国成人网络学习者的词汇学习中采用讲故事方法的有效性。"

2）第2、3、4、5句讲述了论文的研究方法，大意为"60名学生参加了实验，实验组 30 人,对照组 30 人。在 30 分钟的教学中,两组分别采用了讲故事的方法和死记硬背的方法。两组进行了两次后测,一次在教学后立即完成,另一次则在三周后完成。对实验组进行了问卷调查,以获得学习者对讲故事方法的认知。"

3) 第 7、8 句是论文的研究结果和结论,大意为"数据分析结果表明,在短时记忆和长期记忆中,讲故事的方法都比死记硬背更有效,但随着时间的推移,效果趋于减弱。文中提出了完善该方法的建议。"

2.4 引　　言

论文的引言部分主要用来描述当前论文的研究背景,特别需要指出当前研究的必要性,当前研究和已有研究之间的差异等。有的论文作者会直接将文献回顾放到这里,当作研究背景的一部分。接下来,我们通过两篇已经刊发在 SSCI 期刊上的论文来对此部分的写作加以说明。

1) 论文 1 (Qian & Clark, 2016)

论文题目:Game-based Learning and 21st century skills: A review of recent research

引言:

Trends in educational research indicate an increasing interest in how games may influence learning (e. g. , Ke, 2009; Kebritchi, Hirumi, & Bai, 2008; Wu, Chiou, Kao, Hu, & Huang, 2012b). To date, a number of literature reviews have been conducted regarding the effectiveness of game-based learning in various domains such as business, math, statistics, computer science, biology, and psychology (e. g. , Boyle et al. , 2014; Connolly, Boyle, MacArthur, Hainey, & Boyle, 2012; Dempsey, Rasmussen, & Lucassen, 1994; Emes, 1997; Randel, Morris, Wetzel, & Whitehill, 1992; Vogel et al. , 2006; Wolfe, 1997; Wu et al. , 2012b). However, no consensus has been reached in respect to the positive effect of game-based learning. For example, some studies (e. g. , Boyle et al. , 2014; Dempsey et al. , 1994; Randel et al. , 1992; Vogel et al. , 2006) pointed out that game-based learning might be superior to traditional classroom instruction as it could increase students' motivation for learning and provide them with opportunities to explore and acquire new knowledge and skills, but others (e. g. , Emes, 1997) did not find strong evidence which supports the association between game-based learning and students' high academic achievements or psychological development.

Furthermore, most of the previous literature reviews (e. g. , Connolly et al. , 2012; Emes, 1997; Ke, 2009; Randel et al. , 1992; Wolfe, 1997; Wu et al. , 2012b) focused on the statistical significance of empirical studies and rarely emphasized their practical significance (i. e. , effect size), though the latter is much more informative than the former. Specifically, any test with a large sample size tends to be statistically significant, yet it might not be practically meaningful. Hence, game-based learning may not be more effective than conventional classroom lectures if the comparison appears statistically significant but the corresponding effect size is tiny.

Most importantly, a few studies have indicated that a growing number of researchers are committed to developing educational games to support the teaching of essential 21st century skills (e. g. , Boyle et al. , 2014; Dondlinger, 2007). However, little is known regarding how game-based learning may influence students' 21st century skill development (Ebner & Holzinger, 2007; Ke, 2009; Kim, Park, & Baek, 2009; Papastergiou, 2009; Van Eck & Dempsey, 2002). The 21st century skills refer to a wide range of skills such as learning and innovation skills (i. e. , critical thinking, creativity, collaboration, and communication) and information, media and technology skills (Binkley et al. , 2014), and have been gaining more and more attention from researchers and practitioners (e. g. , Chan & Yuen, 2014; Gee, 2007). For instance, the current school curriculum in Hong Kong clearly emphasizes the importance of students' creativity development, and as a result, teachers are encouraged to develop or adopt innovative teaching methods to foster students' creativity in the classroom (Chan & Yuen, 2014). But at this point, no model exists as to how to best teach the core 21st century skills in schools.

Game design and play require people to be familiar with media and technology, and it also requires people to be creative and critical thinkers, so it has great potential to facilitate students' 21st century skill development. Given the lack of consistent empirical evidence with respect to the effectiveness of game-based learning, this review aims to examine the most recent literature regarding game-based learning and seeks to further understand the influence of games on learning, with a major focus on students' 21st century skill development.

分析:本文题目是《基于游戏的学习与 21 世纪技能:研究综述》。引言的第一段介绍了游戏对于学习的影响。第二段则指出之前关于此类研究的综述多集中在实证研究的统计学意义上,而忽略了实际意义。第三段讲述了目前已经有一些研究用教育游戏的方法来教授学生基本的 21 世纪技能。最后一段则指明了本文的写作目的是"研究相关游戏化学习的最新文献,进一步了解游戏对学习的影响,主要关注学生 21 世纪技能的发展。"这篇论文的引言符合上面提出的引言写作的三个要点:介绍写作背景;指出当前研究的必要性;分析当前研究和现有研究的区别。

2) 论文 2(Sadowski & Lomanowska,2018)

论文题目:Virtual intimacy: Propensity for physical contact between avatars in an online virtual environment

引言:

Interpersonal "social" touch plays a fundamental role in nonverbal communication, particularly in exchanging intimate emotions such as love and sympathy (App, McIntosh, Reed, & Hertenstein, 2011; Morrison, Loken, & Olausson, 2010; van Erp & Toet, 2015), as well as in social affiliation and bonding (Dunbar, 2010). Exchanging human touch is also known to have benefits for socioemotional and physiological functioning, such as increased relationship satisfaction and reduced hormonal and cardiovascular responsiveness to stress (Ditzen et al., 2007; Field, 2010; Grewen, Girdler, Amico, & Light, 2005; Morrison et al., 2010). However, with today's widespread use of information technologies for social interactions, much of everyday human contact is mediated through digital means that rely on different communication parameters. In digitally-mediated interactions, non-verbal cues are primarily communicated through the visual modality, omitting the exchange of touch. Although various haptic devices have been created that can be used to mechanically transmit tactile information and incorporate sensory aspects of touch into digitally-mediated exchanges (Bailenson, Yee, Brave, Merget, & Koslow, 2007; Rantala, Salminen, Raisamo, & Surakka, 2013; Saadatian et al., 2014; Tsetserukou, 2010), this technology has not yet gained traction in popular digital applications (van Erp & Toet, 2015). A more commonly used approach to digitally represent human touch is by visualizing interactions in 3-dimensional (3D) online spaces, such as multi-user virtual worlds, using avatars that approximate human appearance (Gilbert et al., 2014; Lomanowska & Guitton, 2012b; Lortie & Guitton, 2011; Pace, Bardzell, & Bardzell, 2010).

Although the visualization of touch is limited with respect to the type of sensory information being transmitted, visual information provides relevant cues about the social context of touch. For instance, the identity of the interaction partners is related to the degree of touch to different body parts exchanged in typical human interactions (Suvilehto, Glerean, Dunbar, Hari, & Nummenmaa, 2015), and also affects how touch information is encoded by the brain's somatosensory cortex (Gazzola et al., 2012). As well, observing different emotions in facial expressions of others can influence the perception of pleasantness of gentle human touch * Corresponding author. Department of Psychology, University of Toronto Mississauga, Mississauga, ON, L5L 1C6, Canada. E-mail address: anna. lomanowska @ utoronto. ca (A. M. Lomanowska). Contents lists available at ScienceDirect Computers in Human Behavior journal homepage: www. elsevier. com/locate/comphumbeh http://dx. doi. org/10. 1016/j. chb. 2017. 09. 011 0747-5632/© 2017 Elsevier Ltd. All rights reserved. Computers in Human Behavior 78 (2018) 1e9 (Ellingsen et al., 2014). Furthermore, studies in the field of social neuroscience have demonstrated that merely observing someone being touched stimulates similar brain responses as directly felt touch (Bolognini, Rossetti, Fusaro, Vallar, & Miniussi, 2014; Keysers, Kaas, & Gazzola, 2010), even enabling the discrimination of the degree of pleasantness of touch (Morrison, Bjornsdotter, & Olausson, 2011). In light of this research, it is possible that the approximation of non-tactile, visual aspects of human touch through contact between avatars in virtual settings may be relevant as a means of simulating some of the functions and benefits of social touch. However, little is known about the way in which virtual touch is exchanged in typical interactions between avatars. Previous research related to the physical aspects of interactions within virtual environments demonstrates that proximity to other avatars is indeed a factor in the way that avatars position themselves in relation to each other (Lomanowska & Guitton, 2012a; Yee, Bailenson, Urbanek, Chang, & Merget, 2007). The goal of the present study was to specifically examine how virtual physical touch between avatars is expressed in this context.

 To study the interpersonal behavior of avatars, we conducted naturalistic observations in the online virtual environment of IMVU (www. imvu. com). IMVU is a freely-accessible 3D chat room platform composed of thousands of user-generated virtual rooms where users can interact through customizable human-like avatars. IMVU is a popular online virtual destination, with over 50 million registered members, 10 million unique monthly visitors, and 3 million monthly active users across the world, as reported by the company (IMVU

FAQ, 2017). IMVU identifies the age demographic of their core members as young adults between 18 and 24 years old, but also caters to older users (IMVU FAQ, 2017). Previous studies that collected demographic information from users showed that the largest proportion of users (70%) were under 25 years of age (Kress, Getz-Kikuchi, Price, Karanian, & Nass, 2011), but older individuals, including seniors, were also present (Kress et al., 2011; Siriaraya & Ang, 2012). With respect to gender, approximately 60%-65% of polled users identified as female (Kress et al., 2011; Siriaraya & Ang, 2012). A small proportion ($<1\%$) also identified as transgender (Kress et al., 2011). A prominent demographic feature of IMVU is the identification of the user's country of origin in their profile, with approximately 89 countries represented among users at any one time. Overall, IMVU comprises a relatively diverse population of users and provides an attractive environment for the study of natural human interactions in virtual contexts.

Similarly to other well-studied virtual worlds, such as Second Life, the IMVU platform is designed to allow users to choose and customize a 3D avatar, as well as create and decorate virtual spaces by purchasing items from a catalog of user-generated virtual goods. Users can engage in a variety of activities by visiting chat rooms designed according to different themes (e.g., dance clubs, beaches) and socializing within these chat rooms with other users. IMVU also includes social networking features that allow users to create personal profiles and connect with other users across the platform. Although the IMVU platform shares many of the same elements as other virtual worlds, a unique aspect of IMVU is that avatar movements are constrained by pre-determined animated poses available in each chat room. A variety of poses are typically available for users to choose for their avatars, including different body postures such as standing, sitting or lying down, different dynamic features, such as swaying or dancing, as well as interactive features, such as embracing. This aspect of IMVU makes the platform a valuable model to study avatar interactions and lends itself particularly well to precise and reliable observation of instances of avatar physical contact. We took advantage of these features of IMVU to examine the typical physical interactions that avatars engage in within public online virtual spaces. We focused our observations on the poses that users chose for their avatars within various chat rooms and quantified the type and frequency of poses that represented interpersonal physical contact.

分析：本文题目是"虚拟亲密：虚拟环境中化身之间身体接触的倾向"。引言第一段的大意是：人与人之间的身体接触是传达亲密关系的一种非语言途径。随着信息技术的发展，很多人利用虚拟环境中的虚拟化身进行交流。第二段指出虚拟环境中的化身之间的接触可能反映了现实中的社交接触的某些功能。但是，对于虚拟环境中的化身之间的交互方式，人们则知之甚少。从而引出当前研究的目的是"研究虚拟环境中的化身之间是如何表达这些身体接触的"。第三段则介绍了一个叫做 IMVU 的在线虚拟环境，这也是当前研究的依托工具。最后一段介绍了 IMVU 和其他虚拟环境的区别。这篇论文的引言相对较长，因为其最后的两段文字其实属于文献回顾，所以在引言之后，该文并没有单独的"文献回顾"一章。

2.5 文献回顾

文献回顾是学术论文的必要部分。一般来说，文献回顾做得不深入、不到位都会导致论文在外审阶段给审稿人留下非常不好的印象，认为作者没有对相关话题进行深入的了解。即使审稿人给了修改的机会，也会让再次修改文献回顾部分。所以，我们在初稿阶段就应该尽可能全面地掌握和论文主题密切相关的现有研究。

文献回顾该怎么进行呢？其实并不难，我们需要紧扣论文的主题（题目）来挑选相关的文献即可。举个例子，如果你写的题目是有关"匿名同伴互评"这一话题，那么在文献回顾部分最好综述一下"同伴互评"以及"匿名互评和不匿名互评"相关文献。此外，在文献回顾的最后，我们还需要指出当前论文和前人论文的区别（这些区别，在引言部分也需要提出，在文献回顾部分可以再次强调一下）。我们来看两篇已经发表在 SSCI 期刊的论文，看看它们的文献回顾是如何进行的。

论文 1（Bahreini, Nadolski, & Westera, 2017）

论文题目：Communication skills training exploiting multimodal emotion recognition
文献回顾：

2. Related work

It is commonly acknowledged that emotions are a significant influential factor in the process of learning, as they affect memory and action (Pekrun, 1992). The influence of emotions on learning is traditionally well recognized in classroom teaching practice (Bower, 1981). More recently, emotions have also received attention in the domain of intelligent tutoring systems （ITS）(Sarrafzadeh, Alexander, Dadgostar, Fan, & Bigdeli, 2008). An ITS is a computer-based system that is capable of providing immediate and personalized instruction and feedback to learners (Psotka & Mutter, 1988). The general premise is that extending ITS with emotion recognition capabilities would lead to better conditions for learning, as it allows for adjusting its interventions to the emotional states of the user. Although there are many studies reported in the wider domains of emotion recognition and ITS, to our knowledge no study has yet been conducted that specifically combines automatic facial and vocal emotion recognition in communication skills training.

An important success factor in classroom learning is the capability of a teacher to timely recognize and respond to the affective states of their learners. For this, teachers continuously adjust their teaching behaviour by observing and evaluating the behaviour of the learners, including their facial expressions, body movements, and other signals of overt emotions. In e-learning, just as with classroom learning, it is not only about cognition and learning, but also about the interdependency of cognition and emotion. These relationships between learners' cognition and emotion are influenced by the electronic learning environment, which mediates the communication between participants (teacher, learner, and his peers) and contains or refers to e-learning materials (e.g. text, photos, audios and videos, and animations). Contemporary, instructional approaches increasingly address emotional dimensions by accommodating challenges, excitement, ownership, and responsibility, among other things, in the learning environment. Software systems for e-learning (e.g. ITS, serious games, personal learning environments) could better foster learning if they also adapt the instruction and feedback to the emotional state of the learner (Sarrafzadeh et al., 2008). Within the scope of ITS, Feidakis, Daradoumis, and Caballe (2011) categorized emotion measurement into three types of tools, which have been described in several previous studies: (1) psychological (Wallbott, 1998), (2) physiological (Kramer, 1991), and (3) motor-behavioural (Leventhal, 1984). Psychological tools are self-reporting tools for capturing the subjective experience of emotions of users. Physiological tools comprise sensors that capture an individual's physiological responses. Motor-behaviour tools for emotion extraction use special software to measure behavioural movements captured by PC cameras, mouse, or keyboard. Most of these emotion recognition tools suffer from limited reliability and unfavourable conditions of use, which hampered successful implementation of so-called affective tutoring systems (ATS). But more recently, there has been a growing body of research on ATS that recommends emotion recognition technologies based on facial expressions (Ben Ammar, Neji, Alimi, & Gouardères, 2010; Wu, Huang, & Hwang, 2015) and vocal expressions (Rodriguez, Beck, Lind, & Lok, 2008; Zhang, Hasegawa-Johnson, & Levinson, 2003).

Communication skills' training typically involves expressing specific emotions at the right point and time; such training can become tedious, as it requires prolonged practice. Serious games offer a challenging and dynamic learning context that seamlessly combine emotion and cognition (Westera, Nadolski, Hummel, & Wopereis, 2008). Such games are characterized by timely feedback to cater for skills learning from prolonged practice and are praised for their motivational affordances (Van Eck, 2010). Note that as online communication is inherently truncated communication, which tends to strip messages from their emotional dimensions (Westera, 2013), emotion recognition is an emerging field in human-computer interaction as this would be a promising next step in enhancing the quality of online interaction and communication. Unfortunately, only a few studies address emotion recognition in digital serious games. A study by Hyunjin, SangWook, Yong-Kwi, and Jong-Hyun (2013) investigated whether a simple brain computer interface with a few electrodes can recognize emotions in more natural settings such as playing a game. They invited 42 participants to play a brain-controlled video game wearing a headset with single electrode brain computer interface and provided a self-assessed arousal feedback at the end of each round. By analysing the data obtained from the self-evaluated questionnaires and the recordings from the brain computer interfaces device, they proposed an automatic emotion recognition method that classifies four emotions with the accuracy of about 66%. Some studies address adaptation in games based on the measurement of user's emotions, motivation, and flow (Pavlas, 2010; Tijs, Brokken, & IJsselsteijn, 2009). In the study conducted by Tijs et al., the researchers investigated the relations among game mechanics, a player's emotional state, and the associated emotional data. The researchers manipulated speed as a game mechanic in the experimental sessions. They requested players to provide their emotional state for valence, arousal, and boredom-frustration-enjoyment. Moreover, they measured a number of physiology-based emotional data features. Then, they compared the previous approaches and found correlations between the valence/arousal self-assessment and the emotional data features. Finally, they found that there are seven emotional INTERACTIVE LEARNING ENVIRONMENTS 1067 data features, such as keyboard pressure and skin conductance that can distinguish among boring, frustrating, and enjoying game modes.

Other studies have shown that it is possible to measure facial and vocal emotions with considerable reliability in real time, both separately and in combination (Bahreini et al., 2015, 2016a, 2016b). Taking this previous research into account, our approach will use common low-cost computer webcams and microphones rather than dedicated sensor systems for emotion detection. First, emotion detection could be used for tracking the learner's moods during their learning, which could inform the pedagogical intervention strategies to be applied for achieving optimal learning outcomes. Second, when emotions are part of the learning content, which is the case in communication skills training, emotion recognition could be used for measuring the learners' mastery of emotions and providing feedback. In this study, we focus on the latter usage of the facial and the vocal emotion recognition technologies. Furthermore, we will revert to the emotion classification suggested by Ekman and Friesen (1978), which is widely used in psychological research and practice. This classification comprises six basic emotions: happiness, sadness, surprise, fear, disgust, and anger. In addition, we will include the complement, neutral emotion.

分析：这篇论文的题目是《利用多模态情感识别进行沟通技能训练》。按照前面提到的文献回顾的写作方法，我们可以根据这个题目来搜索相关文献进行写作。题目的关键点明显包括"情感识别"和"沟通技能"这两个主题，此外，"多模态"也可以作为一个回顾点。我们来具体看看该论文是如何安排文献回顾的吧。

首先，该文用"相关工作"（related work）来表示"文献回顾"，这没什么问题，章节标题只要大体符合意思即可。该部分第一段大意是"情绪是学习过程中的一个重要影响因素，因为它影响记忆和行动。情绪也在智能辅导系统领域（Intelligent tutoring system，ITS）受到关注。然而，现有的研究还没有专门将面部和声音情感自动识别结合应用到交流技能的培训。"很明显，这一段提到了"情绪识别"和"沟通技能培训"这两点，而且还指出了现有研究的不足，从而为当前研究的必要性做铺垫。

第二段大意是"网络学习就像课堂学习一样，不仅关系到认知与学习，而且关系到认知与情绪的相互依赖。学习者的认知和情绪之间的这些关系受到网络学习环境的影响。在学习环境中，教学方法越来越多地通过适应挑战、兴奋、所有权和责任感等方式来解决情绪层面的问题。然而，现有的这些情感识别工具大多数可靠性有限，易受到使用条件的限制，这妨碍了所谓的情感辅导系统（Affective

Tutoring Systems，ATS)的成功实施。但是最近，有关 ATS 的研究越来越多，这些研究推崇基于面部表情和声音表情的情绪识别技术。"可以看出，这一段继续指出现有相关研究的不足，同时，也指出现有研究的发展倾向。

第三段大意是"交流技能的训练通常包括在正确的时间和地点表达特定的情绪，这种训练可能会变得乏味，因为它需要长期的练习。情绪识别是人机交互中一个新兴的领域，这将有利于提高在线交互和交流质量。"这一段讲述了情绪识别在交流技能培训中的潜能。

最后一段大意是"其他研究表明，可以实时测量面部和声音的情绪，无论是单独测量还是组合测量，都具有相当的可靠性。考虑到先前的研究，我们的方法将使用普通的低成本计算机网络摄像头和麦克风，而不是专用的传感器系统来检测情绪。"这一段再一次提到了当前研究和现有研究的不同，指出了当前研究的创新之处。

论文 2（Huisman, Saab, van Driel, & van den Broek, 2018）

论文题目：Peer feedback on academic writing: Undergraduate students' peer feedback role, peer feedback perceptions and essay performance

文献回顾(本文的文献回顾被放在了"引言"部分)：

Introduction

Peer feedback is frequently applied within the higher education context. As an instructional method, it can be beneficial to students' learning of domain-specific skills (van Zundert, Sluijsmans, and van Merriënboer 2010). With respect to the learning mechanisms involved in the peer feedback process, some prior studies have differentiated between providing and receiving peer feedback on academic writing (e. g. Cho and MacArthur 2011; Greenberg 2015; McConlogue 2015; Nicol, Thomson, and Breslin 2014). To our knowledge, however, a direct (quasi-) experimental comparison of the impact that providing versus receiving peer feedback has on students' learning gains is lacking. As a consequence, it remains an open question how these compare in terms of their relative impact on students' writing performance.

The current study has two central aims. First, it compares the effects of providing versus receiving peer feedback on students' performance in the context of an authentic academic writing assignment. Second, to gain more insight into the peer feedback process, it investigates the relations between the nature of the received peer feedback, students' perceptions thereof, and their subsequent writing performance.

Providing versus receiving peer feedback

Providing peer feedback is considered beneficial to students' writing as it stimulates them to actively consider the task-specific processes and criteria. According to Flower et al. (1986), three specific processes come into play when a student reviews a text. First, there is problem detection. Second, there is problem diagnosis, which helps to improve writing when potential revision strategies are not obvious, i. e. do not involve relatively straightforward corrections or rewriting. Third, strategies for revision concern actions that follow problem detection and diagnosis. The act of providing peer feedback triggers students to engage in problem detection, and can stimulate them to engage in problem diagnosis and subsequently contemplate solutions and suggest revisions. As a result, students who provide peer feedback gain experience in problem detection, may become more aware of (types of) writing problems, and may discover different revision strategies (Patchan and Schunn 2015). These feedback processes include students taking different perspectives, comparing others' work to their own and the assimilation of new knowledge, which can be coherently referred to as reflective knowledge building (e. g. van Popta et al. 2017; Tsui and Ng 2000).

Two quantitative empirical studies have provided support for such learning-by-reviewing with academic writing (Cho and MacArthur 2011; Greenberg 2015). Cho and MacArthur (2011) found that students who reviewed three example papers performed better on a subsequent writing task compared to both students who only read these same example papers and to controls reading papers on an entirely different subject. Greenberg (2015) also found that students improved their research reports after providing peer feedback, and this improvement was evident across both simple and more complex sections of their reports. Yet, neither of these studies directly compared the impact of providing versus receiving peer feedback on students' final writing performance. To our knowledge, such a comparison has only been reported by Lundstrom and Baker (2009). They found that lower proficiency 'givers' outperformed lower proficiency students in a 'receiver' condition. In this particular study, however, students' experience of providing versus receiving (utilising) peer feedback was restricted to a controlled training intervention, without them actually providing or receiving peer feedback on each other's writing.

In summary, none of these studies directly compared the impact of providing versus receiving peer feedback in the context of an authentic writing task. As authentic writing tasks concern selfgenerated texts and may affect students' grades, students may be inclined and incentivized to provide peer feedback and respond to received feedback more seriously (McDowell 2012). Qualitative inquiries in authentic contexts indicate that students can perceive the benefits of providing peer feedback (Chen 2010), and that they may even consider this more beneficial to their learning than receiving feedback from peers (Ludemann and McMakin 2014; McConlogue 2015; Nicol, Thomson, and Breslin 2014). The current study's first central aim is to compare the impact that providing versus receiving peer feedback has on students' academic writing performance.

Research question 1: To what extent do students who provide peer feedback improve their writing compared to students who receive peer feedback?

Students providing peer feedback are expected to improve their writing at least as much as students receiving peer feedback. If this expectation is confirmed, this would support the learning-by-reviewing rationale. In contrast, if students receiving peer feedback outperform those providing it, this would indicate that the learning mechanisms involved in the act of providing peer feedback are not as strong as those involved in receiving and utilising peer feedback (e.g. receiving information on the gap between current performance and goal performance; Hattie and Timperley 2007; Nicol and Macfarlane-Dick 2006).

Student perceptions of received peer feedback

The second central aim of the current study is to investigate the relation between the nature of the received peer feedback and students' perceptions thereof, and the relation between these perceptions and subsequent writing performance.

The nature of the peer feedback message

The current study focusedon task-level peer feedback, adopting the operationalization proposed by van den Berg, Admiraal, and Pilot (2006). This operationalization differentiates between the aspects of the text on which the feedback focuses (including content, structure and style) and the functions of the feedback (including analysis, evaluation, explanation and revision). There were three reasons for adopting this operationalization. First, the four feedback functions by van den Berg, Admiraal, and Pilot (2006) are largely consistent with the different feedback functions and components described in prior review studies. For example, evaluations, explanations and suggestions for revision mirror a conceptual resemblance with 'correcting' and 'guiding' (Narciss 2008), and relate to the questions of how a student is doing in relation to the standard and how to proceed towards that goal (Hattie and Timperley 2007). Second, we considered the inclusion of van den Berg, Admiraal, and Pilot's (2006) feedback aspects content, structure and style as a valuable addition to the feedback functions, as we expected these feedback aspects to be relatively salient to students. For example, we expected that students will differentiate between the value of relatively superficial peer feedback on writing style or grammar versus more content or structure related peer feedback. Third, the operationalization of feedback aspects closely aligned with the criteria of the essay assignment that was the subject in this study.

Student perceptions of peer feedback aspects and functions

The relation between the nature of the peer feedback and subsequent writing performance is likely to be mediated by students' perceptions of the received peer feedback (Strijbos, Narciss, and Dünnebier 2010). However, empirical inquiries into students' perceptions tend to focus on students' general experience of the peer feedback process (e. g. Mostert and Snowball 2013). This study contributes to the existing literature by investigating the relations between the nature of the received peer feedback, students' perceptions thereof, and subsequent writing performance. To this end, we used the feedback-perception questionnaire developed by Strijbos, Narciss, and Dünnebier (2010). This questionnaire measures students' perceptions regarding the adequacy of the received peer feedback and their willingness to improve based upon it. In particular, we wish to assess the extent to which peer feedback on particular aspects of the text (content, structure or style) and with particular functions (analytical, evaluative, explanatory or suggesting revisions) relates to students' perceptions of adequacy and their willingness to improve.

Regarding the peer feedback aspects, comments on content and structure are more likely to go beyond straightforward corrections or rewriting than comments on style, and, therefore, are expected to stimulate more substantial revisions. Prior research indicates that complex revisions predict subsequent writing quality (Cho and MacArthur 2010). If students can recognise the different peer feedback aspects and, at least to some extent, differentially value the potential contributions of these aspects in making substantial revisions, then it seems plausible to expect that peer feedback on content and structure will be perceived as more adequate than peer feedback on style.

Regarding the peer feedback functions, these - implicitly or explicitly - indicate discrepancies between students' current performance and the performance goal of the task (analysis, evaluation), provide suggestions on how to advance towards that goal (revision), and provide explanatory information on either the gap between current and goal performance or the suggested revision (explanation) (Hattie and Timperley 2007; Lizzio and Wilson 2008). As a result, we expect these peer feedback functions to positively relate to students' perceptions of adequacy and their willingness to improve.

Research question 2: To what extent do students perceive peer feedback on aspects of content and structure as adequate compared to peer feedback on aspects of style?

Research question 3: To what extent are perceived peer feedback adequacy and students' willingness to improve related to the degree in which the peer feedback is analytical, evaluative, explanatory or suggesting revisions?

Peer feedback perceptions and writing performance

Students' perceptions may mediate between the received peer feedback and subsequent performance (e.g. van der Pol et al. 2008; Strijbos, Narciss, and Dünnebier 2010). It clearly is important to understand how such peer feedback perceptions relate to students' subsequent writing performance in authentic learning contexts. It is to be expected that students' perceptions of adequacy and their willingness to improve based upon the received peer feedback positively relate to their subsequent writing performance. However, empirical evidence for such perceptions/performance relations is mixed. van der Pol et al. (2008) found that students were more inclined to use peer feedback for revising their work when they regarded the peer feedback as important. In contrast, Strijbos, Narciss, and Dünnebier (2010) did not find a relation between students' peer feedback perceptions and revision efficiency (including error detection, error diagnosis and correctly suggested revisions) in a controlled experimental setting. In the context of a more authentic online peer assessment task, Kaufman and Schunn (2011) also found no relation between student perceptions and the frequency of revisions made. Focusing on students' writing performance instead of revision, the current study investigates the relation between peer feedback perceptions and writing performance within an authentic academic writing assignment.

Research question 4: For students receiving peer feedback, to what extent do perceived adequacy and willingness to improve relate to their subsequent writing performance increase?

A positive relation between, on the one hand, perceived peer feedback adequacy and/or students' willingness to improve, and, on the other hand, students' subsequent writing performance would support the findings by van der Pol et al. (2008). Moreover, if peer feedback in relation to certain aspects of the text or serving a particular function relates to these peer feedback perceptions (research questions two and three), this would shed light on how the nature of peer feedback influences students' writing performance. In contrast, if students' peer feedback perceptions do not relate to their subsequent writing performance, that would be in line with prior studies by Strijbos, Narciss, and Dünnebier (2010) and Kaufman and Schunn (2011). This would suggest alternative pathways through which the reception of peer feedback may influence subsequent writing performance, such as through inducing reflection (cf. Kaufman and Schunn 2011). See Figure 1 for an overview of the research questions.

分析：本文题目是《学术写作中的同伴反馈：大学生同伴反馈中的角色、同伴反馈感知与论文成绩》。从文章题目可以知道，该论文的关键点在于"学术写作""同伴反馈""同伴反馈中的角色"和"同伴反馈的感知"等几个方面。本文的文献回顾被放在了"引言"部分。接下来，我们具体分析此部分的写作特点。引言的第一段介绍了同伴反馈在高等教育中的应用，这明显属于论文背景部分；第二段介绍了当前论文的写作目的。

后面的部分都属于文献回顾，作者又用小标题分为：1) 提供与接收同伴反馈；2) 学生对收到的同伴反馈的看法；3) 同伴反馈的感知与学术写作成绩。其中，第二小节又分为"同级反馈的本质"和"学生对同伴反馈各方面和功能的看法"两个部分。我们可以看出这几个部分围绕的焦点与论文题目所透露出的焦点是一致的。

在"提供与接收同行反馈"这一小节，作者大意是"提供同伴反馈被认为有益于学生的写作，因为它鼓励他们积极地考虑特定任务的过程和标准。但是，现有的研究很少直接比较在真实写作任务中提供与接受同伴反馈的这两种不同角色对写作的影响。"这明显是为了突出当前研究的必要性。

"学生对收到的同伴反馈的看法"这一小节谈到当前研究采用了一个可操作化的方法，并介绍了该方法。此外，还介绍了学生对同伴互评的感知。

"同伴反馈的感知与学术写作成绩"这一小节谈论了学生对同伴反馈的感知可能在收到的同伴反馈和随后的表现之间起调节作用。

通过以上两个例子我们发现,文献回顾部分需要紧扣论文的主题。有时,我们可以用小标题来对文献回顾进行划分,这样会使得文献回顾更有层次感。此外,文献回顾可以安排在引言之后另起一章,也可以融合在引言部分。目前,这两种安排方式都被接受。

2.6　研究问题

在文献回顾之后,我们需要介绍当前论文的研究问题。此部分的写作一般有两种处理方式:第一种是首先再次重复当前文章的研究目的(引言部分一般已经给出研究目的,所以此处是复述一遍,文字上可以稍做变化,不能照搬原句),然后给出相应的研究问题。这种方式适用于绝大部分研究,包括质的研究(Qualitative Research)、量的研究(Quantitative Research)、文献综述类(Review Article)等。第二种处理方式主要针对实证研究。因为实证研究多有实验假设,所以我们可以在研究问题一章列出实验的研究假设(一般可以用零假设的方式)。不过,目前多数研究都是直接用罗列的方式给出几个研究问题,而给出实验零假设之类的处理方式较少见了。下面我们通过两篇具体的论文来看看此部分的处理。

论文1(Huisman,Admiraal,Pilli,et al,2018)

论文题目:Peer assessment in MOOCs:The relationship between peer reviewers' ability and authors' essay performance

研究问题:

Research Questions

The central aim of this study is to explore the extent to which peer reviewers' ability is related to authors' essay performance, and to what extent authors' and reviewers' ability interact. Two research questions are formulated. Research question 1 is: "to what extent is peer reviewers' ability related to authors' essay performance?" Research question 2 is: "to what extent does the ability of authors and peer reviewers interact in explaining authors' essay performance?"

分析:这篇论文的题目是《慕课中的同伴评价:同伴评价者的能力与被评价者论文成绩的关系》。这个题目很明了地告诉读者该论文的研究问题是"同伴评价者的能力会对被评价者论文的成绩有何影响"。我们再来看看这篇论文的"研究问题"一章,该章只有一段文字,第一句介绍了文章的中心目标是"探讨同伴评价者的能力在多大程度上与被评价者的论文成绩相关,以及被评价者的能力与评价者的能力在何种程度上相互作用"。这一段最后一句则是两个研究问题,分别是1)同伴评价者的能力在多大程度上与被评价者的论文成绩有关?2)在解释被评价者的论文成绩方面被评价者的能力和评价者的能力有多大程度的相互作用?可见,这两个研究问题和研究目的基本重合,只不过用罗列的方式更明确地表达了一遍而已。

论文 2（Herodotou,2018）

论文题目:Mobile games and science learning: A comparative study of 4 and 5 years old playing the game Angry Birds

研究问题:

Aim, research questions and rationale

The aim of this study is to capture and analyse the interactions of 4 and 5 years old with the game Angry Birds and report on their impact on science learning and development. Angry Birds is labeled as suitable for all ages yet, given the developmental differences among preschoolers, it was deemed important to examine whether such games are beneficial or not across different preschool ages and whether special attention should be given in testing these games with specific ages and labeling them as appropriate accordingly. Through a comparative study of two groups of children (group 1: 5 years old; group 2: 4 years old), this study aims to answer the following research questions (RQs):

RQ1: *What are young children's preconceptions about projectile motion?*

RQ2: *How do young children's age and general performance relate to playing the game Angry Birds?*

RQ3: *How does playing the game affect scientific thinking about projectile motion?*

Preschool children present basic abilities to engage in scientific thinking that is, reasoning to evaluate evidence and understand experimentation in simple tasks. Preschoolers' scientific reasoning skills appear in the age of 4 in the form of evaluating evidence and understanding experimentation in simple tasks. Sobel, Tenenbaum, and Gopnik (2004) demonstrated that children's causal inferences cannot be explained by mere recognitions of associations among events similar to classical conditioning (conditioned vs. unconditioned stimuli) and/or a calculation of their associative strength (associative strength is translated into causal strength). Rather, causal relationships were explained through probabilistic reasoning by taking into account how the prior probability of the outcome might inform observed data. Sobel et al. concluded that despite the children's inability to explicitly reason about probabilities, they can use probabilistic information to infer causal relationships. By the age of 5 and 6, they can successfully infer causal relationships between variables in the lack of evidence (Piekny, Grube, & Maehler, 2013) in areas such as folk physics (Baillargeon, Kotovsky, & Needham, 1995).

Children start using causal language to describe force relations by the age of 4 which, however, supplement with gestures to form complete causal sentences (Goksun, George, Hirsh-Pasek, & € Golinkoff, 2013). The understanding of simple causes precedes the development of causal language. Goksun et al. examined whether children are able to combine multiple forces and process events in terms of force dynamics before productive talk about causal relationships. Results revealed the children's ability to correctly judge the direction and end point of a single-force trial indicating that children before the age of 5 focus on a single direction when predicting the direction of the movement of objects while after 5 they begin considering secondary dimensions (eg, gravity and inertia, force dynamics).

This line of research suggests that there are substantial differences in scientific thinking skills and understanding of force dynamics between preschool age children in particular 4 and 5 years old which should be taken into account when examining the effects of mobile technologies on preschool age children. Considering this cognitive variation, this study accounted for the age and scientific capabilities of children and made the following hypothesis:

Hypothesis 1: There will be significant differences between 4 and 5 years old in their understanding of projectile motion after playing the game for a period of time.

Children tend to form intuitive theories based on experiential thinking often incorporating a number of misconceptions in their theories. Everyday explanations such as direct observations of phenomena and fragmented stories from adults are prevalent in preschool and affect the interpretation of new information and the development of scientific thinking (Kikas, 2010). Theory-based explanations and misconceptions fade out as children grow older due to executive control over thinking (Gropen, Clark-Chiarelli, Hoisington, & Ehrlich, 2011). Preschoolers have misconceptions about objects' trajectories when more than one causal force are combined. Children (mean age 5) when asked to predict the path of a rolling ball off a table predicted a straight rather than a parabolic line (Hood, 1995). One exemption to this misconception was the preschoolers' ability to predict a straight path as the right path of a ball exiting a curved tube—an understanding that changed when entering primary school (predicted to be a curved path) (Kaiser, McCloskey, & Proffitt, 1986). Children can correctly predict where a ball that rolled off a slanted ramp will be landed at the age of 5-6 indicating a conceptual understanding of the notion of inertia on projectile motion (Kim & Spelke, 1999). Following the above line of research, the following hypothesis is made:

Hypothesis 2: There will be significant differences between 4 and 5 years old in their preconceptions about projectile motion prior to playing the game.

A discrepancy is identified between intuitive knowledge about projectile motion in action and knowledge expressed in explicit judgements (Bertamini, Spooner, & Hecht, 2004). In a number of experiments, Krist, Fieberg, and Wilkening (1993) compared intuitive knowledge about projectile motion in action (the motion of an object as influenced by gravity) with knowledge expressed in explicit judgements in 5-6 years old and adults. In the action condition, participants propelled a tennis ball from a wooden board with adjustable height towards a target on the ground. Distance from target and height of board varied in between trials. In the judgement condition, a speedometerlike rating scale was used to estimate the optimal speed for different height-distance combinations. The majority of preschoolers took into account one dimension only. The integration of both dimensions when calculating optimal speed was found to increase with age. On the contrary, in the action condition, preschoolers achieved similar results as fourth graders and adults when throwing the ball to the target accounting for both the height and distance as affecting optimal speed.

Hypothesis 3: There will be significant differences between 4 and 5 years old in knowledge about projectile motion in action as measured by gaming performance after playing the game for a period of time.

Children from disadvantaged backgrounds are individuals whose personal or social circumstances such as gender, ethnic origin or family background may comprise obstacles to "achieving educational potential (fairness)" (OECD, 2012, p. 2). These children are at a higher risk of facing school problems including, learning difficulties and high dropout rates (OECD, 2012). Preschool educational experiences are crucial for disadvantaged children as they can affect their cognitive and socio-emotional development and potentially impact "longer-term educational, employment and wider social outcomes" including better cognitive and socio behavioral outcomes and lasting effects in early years at school (Sylva, 2010). Technology instruction interventions might be promising in bridging the socioeconomic gap. For example, computer materials were found to improve phonological awareness, word recognition, and letter naming skills for 5-6 years old children at risk compared to printed materials given to their peers (Mioduser, Tur-Kaspa, & Leitner, 2000). Curriculum policy makers consider ICT experiences in early years as important for setting the foundations for ICT efficiency in later years (Siraj-Blatchford & Siraj-Blatchford, 2000). The educational potential of participating children was examined in this study to identify whether mobile learning can better support children with low performance.

Hypothesis 4: There will be significant differences between high and low performing children in understanding projectile motion after playing the game for a period of time.

分析:本文题目是《手机游戏与科学学习:4岁与5岁儿童玩愤怒的小鸟游戏的比较研究》。我们明显看到,作者将这一章的标题设定为"目的、研究问题和理据"(Aim, research questions and rationale)。从文章的题目我们可以大致猜到文章的研究问题应该是围绕着4岁和5岁的儿童使用"愤怒的小鸟"这款手机游戏对他们在科学学习上的影响有何不同。此外,这部分的斜体字部分表明了文章有三个研究问题和四个研究假设。

三个研究问题分别是:1)儿童对弹射游戏的先入之见(预想)是什么? 2)幼儿的年龄和一般表现与玩"愤怒的小鸟"这款游戏有何联系? 3)这款游戏是如何影响儿童对弹射游戏的科学思维的?

四个研究假设分别是:1)玩了一段时间后,4岁和5岁儿童对弹射游戏的理解将有显著差异;2)在玩游戏之前,4岁和5岁儿童对弹射运动的先入之见存在显著差异;3)游戏进行一段时间后,4岁和5岁的儿童对弹射游戏的认知将表现出显著差异(显示在游戏成绩上);4)玩了一段时间后,高水平儿童与低水平儿童对弹射游戏的理解会表现出显著差异。

我们可以看到,作者给出的四个研究假设并非是零假设(Null Hypothesis),而是零假设的对立面——备择假设(Alternative Hypothesis)。这在论文写作中都是可以接受的。

以上两种研究问题的写作方式在SSCI期刊中频频出现,我们可以根据自己论文的本质进行选择。目前,常见的方式是在陈述论文的研究目标后直接列出论文的几个研究问题,而研究假设则经常被省略。

2.7 研究方法

论文的研究方法部分,在英语中经常用 Method 或 Methodology 来作标题。Method 的中文意思是"方法",而 Methodology 的中文意思是"方法论",所以如果用 Methodology 作标题的话,文章需要讲述研究方法所依赖的深层次的理论依据。

由于学术论文的类型有多种,如实证研究、文献综述等,所以在"研究方法"这一章,具体的内容会有所区别。但是无论怎么写,在"研究方法"这一章都需要陈述清楚论文中牵涉的实验或文献搜集是怎么完成的。对于实证类研究,我们要讲清楚参与者是如何挑选的,如何对参与者进行分组,采用了哪些实验材料和工具,实验的过程是什么样的。对于综述类研究,我们要给出文献挑选的范围、文献检索的公式、文献剔除的标准等。接下来,以两篇已发表的论文为例,我们看看这一部分的写作格式。

论文 1(Lin,2018)

题目:Anonymous versus identified peer assessment via a Facebook-based learning application: Effects on quality of peer feedback, perceived learning, perceived fairness, and attitude toward the system

研究方法:

3. Methods

3.1 *Experimental design and participant*

A two-group experimental research design was employed to examine the effects of anonymous online peer assessment, within a Facebook-based learning application, on 1) the distributions of cognitive, affective and metacognitive peer feedback, and 2) the participants' perceived learning, perceived fairness, and attitude toward system. All participants were randomly assigned to either an anonymous condition, in which assessors' identities remained hidden throughout the peer-assessment process, or an identifiable condition, in which assessors' full real names could be seen by their assessees.

A convenience sampling method was used for this study. A total of 32

Taiwanese undergraduate students who had enrolled in a three-credit-hour teacher-training course that prepares students to teach adult learners were recruited. Of these, 16 participants were randomly assigned to the experimental group (i. e., the anonymous condition) and the other 16 to the control group (i. e., the identifiable condition). Of the 32 participants, 23 (71.9%) were female and nine (28.1%) were male, with 28 participants (87.5%) drawn from the same major, and four (12.5%) from other majors. Moreover, 28 (87.5%) were sophomores, one (3.1%) was junior, and three (9.4%) were seniors and above. 26 participants (81.3%) reported to have used FB for more than two years while six (18.8%) for more than one year, but less than two years. During recent half year, 17 (53.1%) have used FB for more than two hours per day, 12 (37.5%) for more than one hour, but less than two hours, 2 (6.3%) for more than 30 min, nut less than one hour, and 1 (3.1%) for less than 30 min. Hence, the results suggest that most participants already had familiarity with and regularly used FB. The participants received extra credit in exchange for completing the surveys.

3.2 *Experimental procedure*

The last six class sessions of the experimental courses were devoted to a final teaching project which provided the context and content for the current study. This final project required all the participants to conduct a micro-teaching demonstration session, based on their own micro-teaching lesson plan and teaching materials they had created. In each class session covered by the study, five or six participants performed their 20-min demonstrations. The course instructor videotaped each demonstration and uploaded the videos to the Online Peer Assessment and Reflection (onPear) system, so that the peer assessors could review them online. The onPear system was developed for the present study as an online learning application within Facebook. It allows learners to review their own and peers' micro-teaching videos and give and receive peer feedback about their micro-teaching performance and writing of reflective pieces about their teaching. After completing his or her micro-teaching demonstration, every participant received peer feedback from five student assessors, who were randomly chosen from among the same experimental condition's other participants. The student assessors had to input written feedback for their respective assessees on the onPear system within one week. Another requirement of the online peerassessment process was that the assessors had to note a precise time range (a beginning time and an ending time) corresponding to every video clip that they commented on, to demonstrate that they had actually reviewed their assessees' videos. In the week before the study commenced, the course instructor clearly explained the online peer-assessment process; its eight assessment dimensions (i.e., teaching content, teaching materials, teaching media, teaching process and strategy, teacher-student interaction, classroom management and atmosphere, and assessment used in the micro-teaching); examples of each of these dimensions; and the assessment criteria to be used by peer assessors. The use of the onPear system was also demonstrated to the participants at this time. Lastly, in their final class sessions, all participants were asked to complete the surveys described in the following section.

3.3 *Data collection and measures*

The survey instrument consisted of three parts, designed to measure 1) perceived learning from peer assessment, 2) the perceivedfairness of peer comments, and 3) attitudes toward the onPear system. Participants were asked to rate the survey items on a 6-point Likert scale ranging from 1 (strongly disagree) to 6 (strongly agree).

3.3.1 *Perceived learning*

Nine items, previously proposed in Lin (2016), were used to assess students' self-reported perceptions of how much they had learned from peer assessment. This section comprised two subscales: perceived learning from teaching reflection (six items) (e.g., "Peers' comments help me understand the strengths of my teaching"), and perceived learning about teaching competency (three items) (e.g., "Overall, peer assessment helps me learn how to teach"). Lin (2016) found that the two subscales were factorially distinct, with Cronbach's alpha coefficients of 0.91 for the full survey, 0.91 for the subscale of perceived learning from teaching reflection, and 0.86 for the subscale of perceived learning about teaching competency.

3.3.2 *Perceived fairness*

The perceived fairness of peer comments was determined using a modified version of Panadero et al. (2013) single-item scale: "Peer comments I received from peer assessment were not fair enough." Due to the negative wording of this item, the present study reverse-scored it so that high scores on the item indicated high levels of perceived fairness.

3.3.3 *Attitude toward the system*

Six statements were used to measure students' attitudes toward the online peer-assessment system. These statements were: "It was convenient to use onPear for the peer assessment activities"; "onPear let me increase the frequency with which I read peer comments"; "onPear helped me feel that the peer-assessment learning activities were interesting"; "After logging in to Facebook, I often entered onPear to read peer comments"; "I think it was appropriate to use onPear for peer-assessment learning activities"; and "I liked to use onPear for peer-assessment learning activities."

3.3.4 *Peer feedback*

Assessors' written feedback messages were extracted from onPear. Each assessor wrote a feedback message to each of five assessees regarding their micro-teaching performance. Because eight assessors did not submit all five of the required feedback messages, none of their feedback was included into the subsequent content analysis. A total of 120 feedback messages, 60 from the anonymous group and 60 from the identifiable group, were coded and prepared for analysis.

3.4 *Data analysis and coding scheme*

The survey data were examined for outliers and normality. Principal component analysis (PCA) was used to examine the construct validity of the survey regarding attitudes toward the system, and Cronbach's alpha coefficients were used to examine the reliability of all the instruments. In addition to an examination of descriptive statistics, the current study applied separate independent samples t-tests to examine the effect of anonymity on the research constructs. Finally, content-analysis techniques were applied within a three-dimension framework (affective, cognitive and meta-cognitive feedback categories). Following Cheng et al. (2015), the affective category included both support and opposition.

Adapted and modified from Yu and Wu's (2013) study, the cognitive category consisted of identification of teaching strengths and/or weaknesses, vague suggestions for improvement, the "extension" type of explicit suggestions for improvement, and the "critique" type of explicit suggestions for improvement. The meta-cognitive category, adapted and revised from Tsai and Liang (2009), consisted of identification of evaluation, planning, regulation, and reflection. Additionally, one more category — labeled "other" — was created to cover comments that described teaching behaviors and atmosphere, as well as those describing assessors' personal learning experiences that resulted from their assessees' teaching. Table 1 shows the coding scheme used to classify feedback content into these four categories.

The content of a feedback message was analyzed based on the idea(s) it contained. However, just as each feedback message might represent more than one idea, each idea might be classified into more than one feedback category. The primary investigator and a research assistant coded 12 feedback messages, first individually and then jointly, and discussed any instances of disagreement to clarify and refine the coding scheme. To ensure inter-rater reliability of the coding, another 12 feedback messages was coded by the two coders separately. Holsti's (1969) reliability formula was used, due to the open-ended nature of the content features of peer comments. The percentage of agreement between the two coders was 70.24%, which was considered adequate (Tian & Robinson, 2014). Then, descriptive statistics, including frequency and percentage analysis, were used to describe the extent to which the experimental and control groups collectively and individually provided affective, cognitive, and meta-cognitive comments. Lastly, a series of chi-square tests was used to determine the levels of differences between the two groups' peer feedback in each category and its sub-categories.

分析:本文题目是《通过基于facebook的学习应用程序进行匿名与识别的同伴评估:比较两种同伴评估方式对同伴反馈质量、感知到的学习、感知到的公平和对系统态度的影响》。只看这个题目,我们就能大致猜到此研究应该牵涉到对比试验。接下来,我们来具体看看它的"研究方法"一章的写法。

该文"研究方法"被分成了四个小节,分别是:1)实验设计和参与者;2)实验步骤;3)数据收集和测量;4)数据分析和编码方式。

在第一小节"实验设计和参与者"里,作者表示该论文采用了两个小组的实验设计,参与者被随机分配到匿名同伴评审组或者非匿名同伴评审组。实验的目的是检验匿名与否对认知、情感和元认知同伴反馈的分布的影响,以及对参与者感知到的学习、公平感和对系统的态度的影响。参与者的分组采用便利抽样方式(Convenience Sampling),共有32名台湾本科生参加了一项3学分的教师培训课程,该课程是为这些参与者以后进行成人学生的教学做好准备,其中的16名学生被指派到实验组(Experimental Group,匿名同伴评审方式),另外16名学生进入控制组(Control Group,非匿名方式)。

这里需要指出的是,目前多数实证论文在实施的时候,并没有考虑到效应量的问题(Effect Size),这对于实验结果的进一步解读产生了障碍,因为如果效应量太小的话,即使实验结果达到了显著水平,也意味着实验处理方式的实用价值不高。为了解决这一问题,我们可以利用某些软件在实验之初进行一些推算,保证一定的效应量。这里给大家推荐一款免费的软件 G*power,该软件可以在以下网址下载:https://www.psychologie.hhu.de/arbeitsgruppen/allgemeine-psychologie-und-arbeitspsychologie/gpower.html。同时,在该网址也可以下载该软件的使用说明。为了保证实验达到一定的效应量,我们可以利用该软件计算出需要进入实验的最小样本量。图 2-3 所示为利用该软件计算独立样本 T 检验设计方案时需要纳入的最小样本量。我们看到,效应量被设置为 0.5,I 类错误值(Type I error,α)设置为 0.05,检验功效(Power)设置为 0.8,此时计算出来的最小样本量是 128 人,即两组分别需要 64 名参与者。

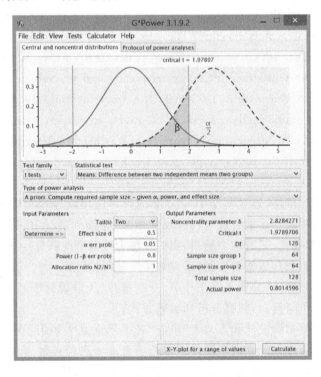

图 2-3　G*power 计算独立样本 T 检验的最小样本量

第二小节"实验步骤"部分详细介绍了该实验的过程,大致如下:实验课程的最后 6 节课被用来开展实验。实验要求所有参与者根据自己的微型课程计划和制作的教学材料,举办一次微型教学示范课。在本实验的每堂课中,5～6 位参与者进行了 20 分钟的演示课程。教师为每节演示课录了像,并将视频上传到在线同伴评估系统(onPear),以便同伴评审员在网上对这些视频进行审查。onPear 系统是为本研究开发的一个在线学习应用程序,可以用于 Facebook 中。该系统使学习者能够审查自己和同伴的微型教学视频,对同伴的教学表现进行评估并接收同伴对自己的教学发表的评审意见。每个参与者都收到了来自 5 位同伴评审员的反馈。同伴评审员是从相同实验条件下的其他参与者中随机挑选出来的。同伴评审员须在一星期内在 onPear 系统里上传对被评审人的教学提出的意见。在线同伴评审的另一项要求是,评审员必须在评论的每一段视频剪辑中注明精确的时间范围(起始时间和结束时间),以证明他们确实审查了被评审人的视频。在实验开始的前一周,课程讲师向参与者清楚地解释了在线同伴评审的过程,评审包括 8 个(注:此处原文应是笔误,应该是 7 个)评估维度(即教学内容、教材、教学媒体、教学过程和策略、师生互动、课堂管理和氛围、微型教学中使用的评测);每个维度的示例;以及同伴评审员使用的评估标准。同时,课程讲师还向与会者演示了 onPear 系统的使用情况。最后,在本实验的最后一节课里,所有参与者需要填写本章下一节所描述的各个问卷。

第三小节"数据收集和测量"又分为四个部分,分别是:1)采用 Lin(2016)年提出的一个包含 9 个题目的问卷,针对的是参与者从同伴评审中获得的知识;2)采用并修订了 Panadero et al. (2013)提出的一个包含 1 个题目的问卷,针对参与者对同伴评审公平性的感知;3)一个包含了 6 个题目的问卷,针对参与者对在线评审系统的看法;4)评审员的反馈信息是从 onPear 系统提取出来的。每一位评审员都会为 5 名被评审人提供评审信息。由于 8 名评估人员没有提交所要求的 5 条评审意见,因此他们的反馈没有被纳入随后的内容分析。最后,研究者共对 120 条评审信息进行了编码,其中 60 条来自匿名组,60 条来自非匿名组。

第四小节"数据分析和编码方式"主要描述了对得到的数据采用何种处理方式。本小节的大意是:问卷数据的异常值和正态都得到了检验。主成分分析法(Principle component analysis)被用来检测对评审系统的态度这一问卷构念的效度(validity)。Cronbach's alpha 系数被用来检验所有调查工具的信度(reliability)。除了描述性数据之外,本研究还针对匿名对研究构念的影响进行了独立样本 T 检验(independent samples T-tests)。最后,论文在一个三维框架(情感、认知和元认知这三类反馈)中应用了内容分析技术(content-analysis techniques)。

本文的认知范畴是从 Yu 和 Wu(2013)的研究中改编而来,包括对教学优点/缺点的识别,对改进的模糊建议和对改进的明确建议属于何种"延伸"类型,以及对改进提出的明确建议属于何种"评判"类型。本文的元认知范畴改编自 Tsai 和 Liang(2009)的研究,包括对评价、计划、规范和反思的识别。此外,论文还添加了一个标记为"其他"的范畴,包括对教学行为和氛围的评论,以及对评审员从被评审者教学视频中获得的学习经验的评论。

此外,论文对评审员的反馈信息进行了内容分析。主要调查员和研究助理对 12 条反馈信息首先进行了独自编码,然后进行了合作编码,并对不一致的地方进行了讨论以澄清和完善编码方案。为了保证评分者信度(inter-rater reliability),

这两名编码者分别又对另外 12 条反馈信息进行了编码。两位编码者的一致性达到 70.24%，这被认为是符合要求的(Tian & Robinson, 2014)。描述性统计数据(频率、百分比)被用来描述实验组和控制组提供的情感、认知和元认知的评审反馈。最后，论文使用了一系列的卡方检验来确定两个小组的同伴反馈在各类别和子类别中的差异程度。

通过对这篇论文"研究方法"的详细分析，我们可以看出"研究方法"这一章的写作方法就是"细致、全面"。该部分必须对参与人员的抽样、分组、实验工具和实验步骤进行细致、全面的叙述。

论文 2(Papadakis, Kalogiannakis, & Zaranis, 2018)

题目：Educational apps from the Android Google Play for Greek preschoolers: A systematic review

研究方法：

4. The research

4.1 *The purpose of this study*

The purpose of this study was to examine whether the educational Apps with Greek content for Android mobile devices contain developmentally appropriate practices to promote preschoolers' optimal learning and development in formal and informal settings, as well as whether they are appropriate in terms of content and design.

4.2 *Sample selection criteria*

During the selection phase, the researchers considered the international literature (Chau, 2014; Goodwin & Highfield, 2012; Handal, El-Khoury, Campbell, & Cavanagh, 2013; Richards, Stebbins, & Moellering, 2013; Shuler, 2012; Watlington, 2011) to produce comparable results with similar international studies in educational Apps with English content. The following criteria were used to select the sample: the Apps had to:

- Belong to the educational category for preschoolers.
- Be available for free, trial or freemium version.
- Be compatible with the Android operating system. The apps did not need to run on the latest edition of the operating system, which during the period of the study was the Android 7.0 Nougat.
- Be available in Google's App store during the selection phase (December2016).
- Contain Greek content.

- Be capable of being installed in both smartphones and tablets (this feature was not a necessary condition).

The Android operating system (Google) was selected instead of the competitive iOS (Apple), because, according to official figures, Android is the most popular operating system for smart mobile devices in the world, with a usage rate of 87.6% for the second quarter of 2016, and this increasing trend is likely to continue (International Data Corporation, 2016). In Greece, similarly, Android has become the most popular mobile operating system (Vodafone, 2016), and there are several smart mobile devices available on the market at all price ranges, as opposed to devices using competing operating systems.

In the aforementioned studies, the mean average number of applications per study ranged between 19 and 240. In the present study, initially, there was no limit on the number of Apps that could be selected for evaluation. But, a thorough search on the Google Play store with the combined criteria (Category: "Education" or "Family" and "Age 5 and below" and content: "Greek") gave rise to a selection of approximately 60 Apps. Ultimately 40 Apps were evaluated. The main reason 20 Apps were excluded from the analysis was that the researchers observed that several of these were identical, as they had the same design, plot, and goals and differed mainly in their appearance using different colour themes. Many Apps offer the same content with just a slightly different audio visual presentation (Notari et al., 2016). Also, several apps by a Greek research institute were excluded as the researchers considered that the low quality of these Apps, might significantly alter the assessment results.

4.3 *The assessment tool*

The REVEAC scale (Rubric for the EValuation of Educational Apps for preschool Children) was used as an assessment tool (Papadakis et al., 2017). This scale differs from others in the literature in that it not only focuses on pedagogical or technical characteristics of an App, or even a single company's products, but also considers the multidimensional aspects of an educational App, as well as the peculiarities of the technological device. The rubric is not only designed to assess the educational value of an App, but also to evaluate several additional features, such as, the amount of information provided to the parents during, and on completion of the App, the configuration options of the App, the degree to which an App can affect a preschooler's cognitive progress, etc. It also considers the existence of advertisements which may disrupt the user's attention, as well as the promotion of electronic transactions (in-app purchases). In summary, the REVEAC assesses the educational apps in the following four domains: educational content, design features, functionality and technical characteristics. The rubric has a high level of internal consistency (Cronbach alpha=0.79) and an average inter-rater reliability of 0.72. The correlations between scale individual items range from 0.58 to 0.78 and are considered large (Shrout & Fleiss, 1979).

4.4 *Evaluation process*

To check that the rubric score is indeed consistent we used the following procedure. A single researcher, expert in the domain, who was familiar with the process reviewed thesample using the following procedure (see Fig. 2):

1. He/she visited the Google Play store and downloaded the sample Apps.

2. He/she "locked" each app installation by disabling the Apps' automatic updates. The necessary third-party App, Adobe AIR, was installed.

3. He/she recorded the App's star rating and user reviews.

4. He/she dealt (played) with each application until it was completed.

5. He/she evaluated each App using the assessment tool.

A second researcher then again reviewed the sample Apps, along with all notes for general agreement on the App scores (assessment tool) and star rating and user reviews (digital store).

分析：本文题目是《安卓谷歌应用商店里的针对希腊学龄前儿童的教育应用程序：一项系统评价》。看到这个题目中的 systematic review，我们就知道这篇论文属于综述类论文。综述类论文一般需要在研究方法部分介绍文献的纳入标准等内容。我们来仔细看看该文的研究方法部分的写法。

这篇论文的研究方法部分分为四个小节，分别是：1)研究目的；2)样本挑选标准；3)评估工具；4)评估过程。

第一小节"研究目的"大意为：本研究的目的是研究用于安卓移动设备的带有希腊语内容的教育应用程序是否包含适当的发展实践，以促进学龄前儿童在正式和非正式环境中的最佳学习和发展，以及这些应用程序在内容和设计方面是否合适。

第二小节"样本挑选标准"指出，纳入本文分析的教育类应用程序需要符合的标准包括：1)属于学龄前儿童教育范畴。2)提供免费版，试用版或免费增值版。3)与安卓操作系统兼容。这些应用程序不需要在最新版本的操作系统上运行，在研究期间，操作系统的最新版本是安卓7.0。4)在样本选择阶段（2016年12月），可以在谷歌的应用程序商店中找到。5)包含希腊语内容。6)能够同时安装在智能手机和平板电脑上(这个特性不是必要条件)。

在此小节的后面部分,作者还说明了为何没有选择苹果的 iOS 系统,这是因为希腊最流行的移动操作系统是安卓。这部分还指出,研究采用的样本搜索字符串是:Category:"Education" or "Family" and "Age 5 and below" and content:"Greek",结果共得到 60 个应用程序,而最终纳入研究的则是 40 个。20 个应用程序被剔除了,原因在于有些应用程序是相同的,因为它们有相同的设计、情节和目标,只是在程序的主题配色上有所不同。有些应用程序提供的内容是一样的,只是采用了稍有差别的音、视频呈现方式而已。此外,一家希腊研究机构开发的几个应用程序被排除在外,因为该文的研究人员认为这些应用程序的质量低下,纳入文章可能会显著改变评估结果。

第三小节"评估工具"介绍了一个叫作 REVEAC (Rubric for the EValuation of Educational Apps for preschool Children,学龄前儿童教育应用程序评价标准)的评估标准。该标准评估了教育应用程序的四个方面:教育内容、设计特性、功能和技术特征。该标准具有较高的内部一致性(Cronbach alpha 为 0.79),评分者信度达到 0.72。量表各项目之间的相关性为 0.58~0.78。

第四小节"评估过程"介绍了对应用程序进行评估的详细过程。首先,由一名相关领域专家按照以下步骤对应用程序进行评分:1)进入谷歌应用商店下载需要评估的应用程序。2)通过禁用应用程序的自动更新来"锁定"每个应用程序的安装,对必要的第三方应用程序 AdobeAIR 进行了安装。3)记录应用程序的星级和用户评论。4)完整地使用该应用程序。5)利用评估工具对该应用程序进行评分。然后,另一名研究人员再次对这些应用程序进行评分,并且对该应用程序的评分(评估工具)、星级和用户评论(数字商店)给出意见。

上面这一篇综述类论文在"研究方法"一章的写作方法和实证类论文写作方法侧重点是不同的。实证类论文侧重于实验的对象、工具、过程等方面,而综述类论文侧重于文献的挑选、剔除、评估标准等方面。但是不管论文类型如何,"研究方法"这一部分必须十分详细地叙述清楚整个实验或综述的各个方面。这种详尽的写作要求也是为了让读者对整个研究的实际开展有完全的了解,从而为可能的验证研究提供可能。

2.8 研究结果

经过以上章节的铺垫后,我们终于来到了一篇论文的"研究结果"部分了。这一部分可以说是一篇学术论文中最好写的部分。因为,只需要在这一部分原原本本地将实验获得的数据表达清楚即可。对于实证研究来说,这一部分需要给出实验的各种结果数据,如实验组和对照组在前测(pretest)、后测(posttest)或延迟后测(delayed posttest)上的成绩有无显著性差异,调查问卷的信度等。对于综述类论文来说,在这一部分需要给出纳入综述的文献或其他内容在各评估维度上的数据等内容。需要指出的是,在对数据的实际处理中可能会得到很多图表,但我们并不需要将得到的所有图表全部写在这一章里,而只需要将最关键的图表展现即可。在这一章,作者需要对图表中的数据进行解释,而可以将数据表达出的延伸内容放到"讨论"这一章中。当然,有的论文将"研究结果"和"讨论"两个部分融为一章,这样可以边给出结果边进行深入分析。这两种处理方式都是可以的。此外,有的审稿人执着于论文的结果部分和前文列出的研究问题一一对应,所以我们可以按照研究问题逐一写出研究结果。接下来,通过两个具体的例子来看看这一部分的实际写法。

论文 1 (van Ginkel, Gulikers, Biemans, & Mulder, 2017)

题目:Fostering oral presentation performance: does the quality of feedback differ when provided by the teacher, peers or peers guided by tutor?

研究结果:

Results

Table 1 shows the descriptive statistics for all criteria in the three conditions.

Main findings

Firstly, analyses showed that significant differences between the various feedback sources exist for all of the seven quality criteria for feedback ($p<0.01$, see Table 1). Secondly, findings demonstrated that the teacher feedback condition scored significantly higher than the peer feedback condition on all seven quality criteria ($p<0.01$). In addition, the teacher feedback condition scored significantly higher than the peer feedback guided by tutor condition on six of the seven quality criteria of feedback ($p<0.01$), the exception being the criterion specificity of feedback. Finally, analyses revealed that the peer feedback guided by tutor condition scored significantly higher than the peer feedback condition on the following four criteria: specificity of feedback ($p<0.05$), content-related arguments ($p<0.01$), ideal or desired performance ($p<0.01$) and progress from actual to desired performance ($p<0.01$).

分析:本文的题目是《培养口头陈述表现:老师反馈、同伴反馈和老师指导下的同伴反馈,三者的反馈质量有何不同?》根据这个题目,我们可以推测文章要对三种反馈做两两比较。这篇论文的"研究结果"相对简单,只有一张表格,文字解释也较少,这是因为该论文在其上一章"研究方法"里已经详细介绍了数据分析的方法。

从这里我们也可以看出学术论文的大致框架虽然基本一致,但是在实际写法上却可以有所差别。

就这一篇论文的"研究结果"而言,虽然内容不多,但是作者对表格里的数据还是进行了详细的分析。本部分大意为:首先,分析表明,在所有7种反馈质量标准中,不同反馈源之间存在显著差异($p<0.01$)。其次,研究结果表明,教师的反馈在所有7项质量标准上均显著高于同伴反馈($p<0.01$)。此外,在7项反馈质量标准中,教师反馈的得分显著高于教师指导下的同伴反馈($p<0.01$),但反馈的特异性这一标准除外。最后,分析表明,教师指导下的同伴反馈在以下4个标准上得分显著高于同伴反馈:反馈的特异性($p<0.05$)、内容相关的论点($p<0.01$)、理想或期望的成绩($p<0.01$)和从实际成绩到期望成绩取得的进步($p<0.01$)。

论文 2(Hamari & Keronen,2017)

题目:Why do people buy virtual goods: A meta-analysis

研究结果:

3. Results

3.1 *Details of the reviewed studies*

The inclusion process resulted in 20 research papers for further analysis and they are represented in Table 1. When counting also different sub-studies, the total number of studies is 24. The studies have been published between years 2008 and 2015. Majority of the studies are journal articles and the data contains only single conference paper. Sample sizes range from 38 to 2481 with a mean of 529 and standard deviation of 612.

The frequencies of different environment types are shown in Table 2. Twelve studies have been conducted in the context of virtual worlds and 7 studies in the context of games (SNGs: 3, MMOs: 3, and Mobile games: 1) A single did not specify the context.

Most of the studies did report their experiment concerning more than a single service or did not report actual titles of services (7) Among the reported titles, most of the studies did use Habbo Hotel (5), Second Life (3) or Cyworld (3) virtual worlds. Most frequent game title was World of Warcraft but with frequency of only 2. Rest of the reported titles were used in single studies (Table 3).

We also investigated the distribution of theoretical frameworks utilized in the body of literature. As seen in Table 4, our review reveals that majority of the studies did not specify any clear theoretical foundation or used variety of variables from different frameworks or studies. Moreover, use of specific theories and models is rather scattered and only low frequencies are detected. Nevertheless, some studies utilized technology acceptance model (Davis, Bagozzi, & Warshaw, 1989), theory of planned behavior (Ajzen, 1991) and unified theory of acceptance and use of technology (Venkatesh, Morris, Davis, & Davis, 2003).

3.2 *Variables*

In total, the collected data contains large number of different variables and 398 unique correlation pairs. As we were interested in factors that explain virtual goods purchases, we meta-analyzed the correlations between the purchase-related variable and any variables that were featured in at least 3 individual studies. Table 5 introduces the most frequent variables in the reviewed research literature, number of studies examining them (k) as well as a brief description for each variable. These variables are also featured in meta-analysis. Therefore, beyond this meta-analysis, there exists a long-tail of variables that have been investigated in individual studies. Naturally, such a long list is outside the scope of this meta-analysis.

3.3 *Meta-analysis*

3.3.1 *Main findings*

The results in Table 6 (also visualized in Fig. 2) show most frequently studied variables in the literature and our meta-analytically produced estimates for their correlation with Purchase Intention which were in order of magnitude: Attitude (0.662), Flow (0.482), Perceived Network Size (0.480), Self-Presentation (0.478), Subjective Norms (0.466), Social Presence (0.438), Perceived Value (0.418), Service Use Enjoyment (0.370), Service Use Intention (0.359), and Perceived Ease of Use (0.333). Every estimate in the analysis was clearly positive and statistically significant at $p<0.001$ with adequate failsafe N values (See Table 6).

3.3.2 *Moderating effect of service type*

While games and virtual worlds offer purchasable virtual goods, they are relatively different types of environments. Whereas games are commonly competitive, rule-driven, fast-paced goal-orientated and narrative rich, virtual worlds are commonly free-form and have no clearly defined goals or game-like competition. In games, purchasing virtual goods can give unfair competitive advantage as they can make the game character stronger (Alha et al., 2014; Hamari & Lehdonvirta, 2010; Hamari, 2015; Lehdonvirta, 2009). Therefore, the motivations for purchasing virtual goods in these environments may differ.

To address this assumption, we expanded the meta-analysis by investigating the differences between effect between the game and virtual world environments.

Since the number of studies become lowered due to the grouping, we reduced the required k of studies to two for each category. As a result, the comparison analysis compares five relationships between the virtual environment categories (Table 7 and Fig. 3). An asterisk denotes a p-value of lower than 0.05 and in most cases the p-value was lower than 0.01. The results showed a large difference for correlation between Service Use Intention and Purchase Intention ($Q=46.651^*$), where games had considerably lower correlation (0.211^*) compared to mediocre estimate of virtual worlds (0.465^*). Quite similarly, there was a large difference in correlation between Service Use Enjoyment and Purchase Intention ($Q=22.492^*$), where again the relationship for games (0.185^*) was significantly weaker than the estimate for virtual worlds (0.461^*). Moreover, there was slight difference between correlations for Flow and Purchase Intention ($Q=5.920^*$), where games had a lower estimate (0.437^*) compared to virtual worlds (0.557^*). However, the analysis could not detect significant difference for correlation between Subjective Norms and Purchase Intention ($Q=0.052$) since both categories had similar estimates (games: 0.453^*, worlds: 0.494^*). In addition, there was no noticeable difference in relationship between Attitude and Purchase Intention ($Q=0.027$) as both categories showed similarly high correlations (games: 0.666^*, worlds: 0.654^*).

Despite the fact that number of studies is lowered to two studies at minimum, all group estimates are statistically significant and positive. However, in relationship between Subjective Norms and Purchase Intention, correlation estimates for both service categories had wide confidence intervals (see Fig. 3) due to high variation in previous research findings. Games-group had 95% confidence interval of 0.435 whereas virtual world-category had 0.539 in difference between the interval bounds. Although the literature showed rather varying findings on strength of the relationship between the variables, the correlation estimates in this analysis were clearly positive in both categories. Other studies within their categories had rather unanimous results which is shown in relatively narrow confidence intervals (0.245 at most).

分析：本文题目是《人们为什么要购买虚拟商品：一项元分析》。从题目我们可以知道这篇文章还属于综述类论文，而且采用了元分析（又叫荟萃分析，meta-analysis）的综述方法。

再看这篇论文的"研究结果"部分,该部分分为三个小节,分别是:1)纳入综述的研究的细节;2)变量;3)元分析。

第一小节"纳入综述的研究的细节"大意为:本综述纳入讨论的论文有20篇,都是2008~2015年发表的文章,绝大多数是期刊文章,只有1篇是会议论文。这些论文的样本量在38~2481之间。12项研究针对的是虚拟环境,7项针对的是游戏环境,还有1项没有明确说明针对的环境。本综述还研究了文献中使用的理论框架的分布情况。大多数研究没有明确说明其使用的理论基础,或者使用了多种理论框架。此外,特定理论和模型的使用比较分散。然而,也有一些研究采用了技术接受模型、计划行为理论和技术接受与使用统一理论。

第二小节"变量"介绍了这篇元分析综述针对的变量。作者明确指出该综述只针对与购买行为相关的变量和至少在3项研究中都出现的变量之间的相关性进行了元分析。

第三小节"元分析"是这篇论文"研究结果"部分的主要部分,该节又划分成了两个小部分:1)主要发现;2)服务类型的调节效应。该元分析的主要发现是:元分析对几个变量和购买意愿(Purchase Intention)之间的相关性进行了估计,相关性估计值按照大小依次为:态度(Attitude,指自己对购买虚拟服务的正面或负面的态度)(0.662)、沉浸(Flow,指完全沉浸于某一项活动的状态)(0.482)、感知网络大小(Perceived Network Size,指感知到周围有多少家人或朋友也在使用这些虚拟服务)(0.480)、自我呈现(Self-Presentation,指渴望通过虚拟化身等形式在虚拟世界展现自己)(0.478)、主观规范(Subjective Norms,指的是感知到的来自其他人对玩游戏或使用虚拟世界态度的压力)(0.466)、社会存在(Social Presence,指在虚拟世界感知到的人与人之间的真实接触感与社会性)(0.438)、感知价值(Perceived Value,指感知到的虚拟商品的价值与价格的比率,如渴望得到有价值但便宜的虚拟商品,而昂贵的虚拟物品则使用户考虑其他选择)(0.418)、服务使用享受(Service Use Enjoyment)(0.370)、服务使用意愿(Service Use Intention,指有无意愿去玩一项游戏或使用一个虚拟世界)(0.359)和感知易用性(Perceived Ease of Use,指对游戏或虚拟世界在使用中的难度大小的感知)(0.333)。每一个估计值都是显著的($p<0.00$)和有统计学意义的,并且有足够的故障安全值(failsafe value,此值主要是反映元分析的发表偏倚"publication bias"的)。

第三小节的第2部分是"服务类型的调节效应"。该部分大意为:虽然游戏和虚拟世界都可提供虚拟商品的买卖,但是两者的应用环境是不同的。比如,游戏一般有竞争性,而且目的性很强,而虚拟世界通常没有竞争性,也没有明确的目的性。因此,该文又将针对游戏环境和非游戏环境的研究进行了对比。

从以上两篇文章的"研究结果"部分,我们可以看出,不论哪种类型的论文,研究结果部分都需要对数据进行详细的描述。

2.9 讨 论

如果说以上叙述的章节内容都是一篇论文的铺垫的话,那么讨论部分(Discussion)可以说是论文的高潮了,审稿人判断这篇论文有没有贡献,主要就是检阅这一章的写作。在编辑给我们"大修"机会的情况下,很多审稿人的责难都是针对这一章的内容而言。那么,这一部分该如何写作呢?正如上面所说,这一章需要突出自己当前研究的创新点和贡献,所以可以按照以下两点来安排内容:首先,大致总结前一章得到的研究结果(也可以放在论文最后的"结论"一章);其次,指出当前研究在理论(Theoretical implications)和实践(Practical implications)层面提供的创新点(包含当前研究和前人研究的异同点)。正如本书2.8节中提到的,有的论文将"讨论"单独成章,而有的论文则将"讨论"和"研究结果"融为一章,有的论文甚至会把"讨论"和"结论"两章融合在一起。具体写法我们可以通过两个例子来看看。

论文1(Chou, Chang, & Chen, 2017)

题目:Let's draw: Utilizing interactive white board to support kindergarten children's visual art learning practice

讨论:

Discussion

Over the course of the eight learning units implemented in this study, the students were interested in IWB instruction, which directly influenced their learning motivation. This finding was consistent with past research that integrated the IWB into science learning in kindergartens (Linder, 2012; Preston & Mowbray, 2008; Wong et al., 2013). Regarding visual art learning, the finding also supported a previous study that indicated that the IWB might strongly arouse children's learning interest and motivate students to participate in IWB-related learning activities (Terreni, 2011). According to Keller's (1983) motivation theory, stimulating students' curiosity is a critical step in instructional design. In the study, therefore, the IWB served as a novel learning tool for increasing the students' curiosity during the IWB intervention.

In the current study, the joyful learning environment created by IWB instruction obviously facilitated peer discussion and interaction. While volunteers shared their drawings on the IWB, other classmates enthusiastically discussed objects in the drawings and responded to the teacher's queries. Furthermore, after school, the majority of students were eager to share IWB learning scenarios that occurred in their classrooms with their parents, which in turn facilitated social interaction at home. Therefore, the findings in the study echoed the analytical report by Hsin et al. (2014), which stated that ICT positively benefited children's social development when used wisely.

In the study, the IWB enabled students with varied drawing capabilities to construct their individual-based drawings by socially interacting with peers and the teacher in a highly motivated manner. Under such a learning environment, the IWB use in the classroom indeed served as a useful scaffolding tool (Jonassen, 1999; Donohue, 2015) to support learning interaction. In addition, although the quality of the students' drawings did not improve markedly, more diverse and colorful elements appeared in the drawings compared to visual art works in the previous semester. This finding can be attributed to social learning (Bandura, 1977) in children's discussions. The students perhaps observed other styles of visual art and incorporated new elements into their works, which became unique drawings with personal styles.

According to a report from the United Nations Educational, Scientific, and Cultural Organization (UNESCO, 2006), ICT use in schools may support students with special learning needs. For example, ICT can "unlock hidden potential for those with communication difficulties ... [and] enable students to demonstrate achievement in ways which might not be possible with traditional methods" (p. 30). In this study, IWB integration in the visual art curriculum played a critical role in supporting three students who needed more learning attention. Adopting the IWB in the classroom enabled one student with an introverted personality to overcome communication problems, one student with low learning confidence to develop more diverse ideas, and one student with low learning achievement to demonstrate potential learning abilities not shown in a traditional teaching environment. This finding supported a finding from Terreni's (2011) study, which showed that IWB use benefited students with special learning needs in a visual art class.

User experiences reflected the value of technology adoption (Carr-Chellman, 2006). In this study, an IWB mounted on the wall seemed to be a large tablet computer screen on which the students could enjoy working on their drawings. Easy-to-use features in the IWB enabled the students to have new art learning experiences. Some students even perceived the possibility of IWB drawing replacing traditional drawing methods. Although unfamiliar feelings at the initial implementation stage were reported by some students, the user-friendly interface of the IWB still triggered students' learning desire for drawing practice. Therefore, from a practitioner's perspective, IWB adoption in the classroom fitted well with the visual art curriculum. In accordance with Morgan's (2010) observation in UK schools, the IWB was perfectly used to capture students' visual ideas.

Most previous studies tended to focus only on students' learning performances. The role of parents was always a missing component of ICT integration in classrooms. In this study, parents' perceptions were obtained to construct a multi-faceted perspective of ICT adoption (Ravasco et al., 2014). According to the analysis of qualitative themes, several parents identified their children's changed drawing styles. More diverse and colorful elements appeared in the drawings. If IWB instruction is implemented during a school day, children might be eager to share classroom learning stories with their parents after school. Although IWB practice in school might not increase children's drawing frequency at home, most parents appreciated the positive effect of the IWB on children.

From a pedagogical perspective, the IWB was an effective tool for facilitating the teaching process (Wong et al., 2013). However, because the IWB intervention was implemented only in the visual art related curriculum, the visual art teacher was fully responsible for technical preparation of multimedia learning materials. The extra effort required increasing the teaching load for the teacher. This finding was consistent with prior research that indicated that IWB integration in the classroom required an investment of time and effort for the instructors (Smith et al., 2005). Furthermore, when IWB instruction yielded learning benefits for the students, other teachers in the kindergarten began to consider the possibility of technology adoption in their classes. Thus, IWB instruction elicited a relative learning advantage that prompted teachers of other classes to accept ICT adoption (Rogers, 2003).

分析：本文题目是《让我们画画吧：利用互动白板支持幼儿园儿童美术学习实践》，这个题目告诉我们本文的主题是利用互动白板进行幼儿园儿童的美术教学。该文的"讨论"部分包含7个段落，下面我们来仔细分析该部分的写法。

在前5段，作者分析了当前研究的发现，并将这些发现与前人研究的异同进行了比较。这几段大意为：

在本研究实施的8个学习单元中,学生对交互式白板(IWB)的教学产生了兴趣,这直接影响了他们的学习动机。这一发现与过去将IWB纳入幼儿园科学学习的研究是一致的。在美术学习方面,这一发现也支持了先前的一项研究,该研究表明IWB可能强烈地激发儿童的学习兴趣,并激励学生参与与IWB相关的学习活动。根据Keller(1983)的动机理论,激发学生的好奇心是教学设计中的关键一步。因此,在这项研究中,IWB作为一种新的学习工具,可以增加学生的好奇心。

在本研究中,IWB教学所创造的快乐学习环境明显地促进了同伴讨论和互动。此外,放学后,大多数学生渴望与他们的父母分享在课堂上发生的IWB学习情景,这反过来又促进了家庭的社交互动。因此,研究结果与Hsin等人(2014)的分析报告相呼应。该报告指出,如果信息和通信技术使用得当,将积极促进儿童的社交发展。

在本研究中,IWB使具有不同绘画能力的学生能够通过与同学和教师的社交互动这种非常积极的方式来构建他们的个人绘画。在这样的学习环境下,IWB在课堂上就充当了教学支架工具(Jonassen,1999;Donohue,2015),以支持学习互动。此外,虽然学生的绘画质量没有明显提高,但与上学期的美术作品相比,绘画中出现了更多样、更丰富多彩的元素。这可能是因为,学生在学习中观察到了别人的绘画风格,并在作品中加入新的元素,这些元素的加入使他们的绘画具有独特的风格。

在本研究中,IWB在绘画课程中的使用对三名需要更多学习注意力的学生起到了至关重要的作用。在课堂上采用IWB使一名性格内向的学生克服了沟通障碍,使一名学习信心低的学生发展出更多不同的想法,还使一名学习成绩低的学生表现出在传统教学环境中没有表现出来的潜在学习能力。这一发现支持了Terreni(2011)的一项研究,该研究表明,IWB的使用有益于在美术课堂上有特殊学习需求的学生。

在本研究中,安装在墙上的IWB似乎是一个巨大的平板电脑屏幕,学生们可以在上面工作。易用的IWB功能使学生有了新的艺术学习体验。一些学生甚至意识到IWB绘图取代传统绘图方法的可能性。虽然一些学生在最初的实施阶段出现了一些不熟悉的感觉,但IWB的用户界面仍然激发了学生对绘画练习的学习欲望。因此,从美术教师的角度来看,IWB在课堂上的采用与美术课程相得益彰。

第六段,作者分析了之前研究的不足。大意为:以往的研究大多只关注学生的学习成绩,而忽略家长的角色。而本研究获取了父母的意见,从而能站在多个角度来审视在课堂教学中采用ICT(信息与通信技术)这一做法。根据对本文的几大主题的分析,有几位家长发现他们的孩子改变了绘画风格,绘画中出现了更多丰富多彩的元素,而且IWB的使用使得孩子们渴望在放学后与他们的父母分享课堂上发生的学习故事。虽然IWB在学校的使用可能不会增加孩子在家里画画的频率,但大多数家长对 IWB 给孩子产生的积极影响表示赞赏。

在第七段,作者指明了本文的教学实践意义。大意为:从教学角度看,IWB 是促进教学过程的有效工具。然而,由于 IWB 在美术课程中的使用要求美术教师完全负责多媒体学习材料的技术准备,这无疑会增加教师的教学负担。这一发现与先前的研究一致。此外,当 IWB 教学为学生带来学习利益时,幼儿园的其他教师也会考虑在他们的班级中采用这一技术的可能性。因此,IWB 在教学中的应用激发了一种相对的学习优势,促使其他班级的教师接受并采用 ICT 技术。

可以看出,这篇论文的"讨论"部分基本上是紧扣当前论文的结果而提出创新点,同时对当前研究和前人的研究进行了对比。

论文 2(Kordaki & Gousiou, 2016)

题目:Computer card games in computer science education: A 10-year review

结论:

Discussion and conclusions

This work explored CCGs (Computer Card Game) that have been used to support the learning of CS (Computer Science) concepts during the decade 2003-2013 through a review study based on 24 articles identified by using specific search terms. The vast majority of the articles referred to the use of CCG-construction as learning tool in CS tertiary education, with the exception of 4 papers that reported the use of CCG-play as learning tool in lower educational levels or in public use.

Two different approaches to the way CCGs were integrated into the learning process emerged: CCGs as educational game-play tools where students learn by playing the game at hand, or as the artifact of learning where students had to learn computational issues by designing and constructing either the whole game or a part of it based on supportive data they were given by their educators. These findings are congruent with the four approaches suggested by Wallace, McCartney, and Russel (2010).

However, it would appear that CCGs were not only used to motivate and engage students to learn computational issues as it happens when using other types of computer games. In fact, Professors in CS departments recommend the CCG-construction approach due to the inherent logic of this genre of games. It is claimed and verified by empirical data that this logic is suitable for the meaningful learning of various computational issues such as OOP philosophy and principles (e. g. , classes and objects, methods, inheritance, encapsulation, composition, design patterns and polymorphism) as well as networking technologies as social interaction is embedded in CGs-play. It also seemed that a number of CS issues can be learned, through CCG-construction such as: programming, concurrency, database design, SE and AI. It was also emerged that, due to the fact that, CGs are familiar, common and simple games; students, being accustomed to this type of game, can focus on the learning issues without the obstacle of needing to learn the game philosophy. On the other hand, rich, problem solving, social, and constructivist learning experiences have been promoted through CCG-play for the learning of various CS topics such as: binary system, GA, haptic technology, operating systems and software engineering.

The results of the review also show that empirical studies were conducted in less than half of the articles with positive results in terms of learning outcomes and students' attitudes towards the use of ECCGs (Educational Computer Card Game) in the learning process in terms of approval, enjoyment, motivation, and usability. However, more and large-scaled studies are needed to provide more evidence about the learning effectiveness of CCGs.

Modern constructivist views of learning have been also adopted in the use and construction of the ECCGs reported. These views have been mainly implied by the terminology used in most of the reviewed articles. However, it is worth noting that only one of the reviewed articles clearly stated the learning theory that authors followed in the design of their ECCGs. Reflection was attained in most of the reviewed articles and seemed to support the learning process. However, despite the fact that, social interaction is inherent in CG-play only few studies reported collaboration mainly through CCG-construction.

In conclusion, it seems that the construction of CCGs constitutes a meaningful, appropriate and suitable context that has been mainly used in CS tertiary education for the learning of various computational issues, while only a 19 few ECCGs have been suggested as educational, game-play tools. This review study also unfolds interesting perspectives for CS educators, game developers, and students needing further research. The adoption of CCG construction in primary and secondary education to support the learning of CS concepts could also attract the attention of CS researchers and educators. In addition, game designers and developers could be prompted to emphasize the design and implementation of ECCGs so that students might learn various CS concepts through CCG-play. By encouraging students to learn CS subjects early in life, which is attainable within the meaningful and compelling context of CCG-play, they would potentially be inspired to choose careers in the field of CS. All in all, it is hoped that these findings will contribute sufficient information to CS educators and game developers to enable them to be effective users or developers of ECCGs.

分析：本文题目是"计算机科学教育中的电脑卡片游戏：十年回顾"。从这个题目，我们可以知道该文属于综述类研究，我们来看看它的结论部分是如何写作的。

这一部分的标题是"讨论和结论"。很明显，作者将"讨论"和"结论"这两章进行了融合。这一部分共分为六个段落。前五段属于讨论部分，而最后一段则是论文的结论部分。

第一段大意为：本研究探讨了在 2003—2013 年发表的 24 篇针对利用电脑卡片游戏进行计算机知识教学的文章。绝大多数文章都提到在计算机科学高等教育中使用电脑卡片游戏作为学习工具，另有 4 篇论文介绍了在较低的教育水平领域或在科普中使用电脑卡片游戏作为学习工具。

第二段大意为：有两种方法可以将电脑卡片游戏应用到学习过程中。第一种是将电脑卡片游戏作为教育游戏工具，让学生通过玩游戏而学习；第二种是把电脑卡片游戏当作学习的产品，学生通过设计和开发整个游戏的一部分来学习计算机知识。这些发现与 Wallace、McCartney 和 Russel（2010 年）提出的四种方法一致。

第三段大意为：一方面，由于纸牌游戏是一种熟悉的、常见的、简单的游戏，学生在利用这类游戏进行学习时，可以把注意力集中在学习问题上，而不会受到如何进行游戏等问题的影响。另一方面，利用电脑卡片游戏来学习二进制系统、遗传算法等计算机知识可以为学生提供丰富的、解决问题的、社交的和建构主义的学习体验。

第四段大意为：本综述显示，有不到一半的文章进行了实证研究，在学习成绩和学生对在学习过程中使用电脑卡片游戏的态度方面都取得了积极的结果。然而，我们还需要更多的大规模的研究来提供更多的证据以证明利用电脑卡片游戏进行学习的实际效果。

第五段大意为：大多数纳入这篇综述的研究都体现了现代建构主义的学习观。然而值得注意的是，只有一篇论文清楚地阐述了作者在设计电脑卡片游戏时所遵循的学习理论。此外，尽管社交互动是纸牌游戏固有的，但只有很少的研究报道了电脑卡片游戏可以营造合作（collaboration）的氛围。

最后一段是论文的结论部分，大意为：电脑卡片游戏可以应用在计算机科学高等教育中。在中小学教育中采用电脑卡片游戏来支持计算机知识的学习也可以引起计算机科学研究者和教育工作者的关注。此外，游戏设计者和开发人员还可以关注电脑卡片教育游戏的设计和实施，以便学生可以通过此类游戏来学习各种计算机科学的概念。通过利用电脑卡片游戏来学习计算机知识,学生可能会被吸引从而选择计算机科学领域的职业。总而言之,希望这些研究结果能为计算机科学的教育工作者和游戏开发人员提供足够的信息,使他们能够成为电脑卡片教育游戏的受益者或开发者。

从以上的分析,我们可以看出这篇综述性论文在"讨论"这一部分也是紧扣自己研究的重点发现,和前人研究进行对比,从而突出自己的创新点。

2.10 结　　论

"结论"(Conclusions)是一篇论文的收尾部分,一般的处理方式是单独成章,也有作者把"讨论"(Discussion)和"结论"融合在一起作为论文的最后一章。单就"结论"一章来说,作者需要做的就是总结论文的研究目的、研究方法和研究结果。从这一点来说,"结论"和"摘要"部分涵盖的内容基本一致,但是在写作时,我们不要用和摘要完全相同的词句,要尽量做些变化。此外,很多审稿人要求作者在这一章提出论文的局限性(Limitations,也有审稿人要求将局限性放在"讨论"一章,因为那一章会讨论论文的创新点,审稿人认为应该将创新点和局限性放在一起讨论),所以我们可以在"结论"部分加入此类内容。在此基础之上,我们还可以对未来的此类研究提出一些可行的建议。下面我们看两个具体的例子。

论文 1(Mathrani, Christian, & Ponder-Sutton,2016)

题目:PlayIT: Game based learning approach for teaching programming concepts

结论:

Conclusion and future scope

We have applied an innovative way to bring aboutactive learning in classrooms through use of educational games. Suggestions from tutors helped in identifying a subject module considered to be difficult by students. This provided us with an opportunity to apply gaming elements to introductory programming within a classroom environment. Students pursuing a diploma computing course were selected for this study. We applied the game based strategy to one group of students who had no prior knowledge of programming, and to another group who had recently completed the programming module. In this manner, we did not set boundaries to when game based learning should be initiated. Our findings indicate that GBL is a useful learning strategy both before subject is taught and after subject has been taught, but with a slight bias toward after subject has been taught. The GBL experiment showed us that students could be actively engaged in applying programming principles with defined gaming steps. The majority 16 of participating students agreed that gaming approaches to learning can make classroom environments more fun and also make an effective way to grasp some of the difficult concepts.

This study has demonstrated the effective use of GBL as a teaching and learning activity. Students felt confident about practicing theuse of programming constructs in a game scenario and were eager to help others in understanding the game strategy. In applied fields of study such as ICT, the inclusion of gaming elements with traditional teaching practices will bring about more active learning. This will be beneficial for tutors as well as students because games could enable students to grasp technology based applications quickly in a more enjoyable learning environment. This study adds to ongoing teaching and learning pedagogies. This could lead to further research in designing of ICT education curriculum, where learning outcomes of different subject modules could be mapped to related gaming elements, to bring about gradual learning, as games moved from basic (easy) to advanced (complicated) levels.

This study has several limitations. It cannot be said with certainty the effect of GBL with other variables such as the success level, social interactions and self-assessments (Huang & Soman, 2013). Another limitation of this study is that the game (LightBot) covered only an introductory course. Advanced programming would require a more complicated and intensive game. The other limitation is the low response rate in the final paper survey.

The authors believe that traditional classroom teaching cannot be replaced since teachers play both an educator and a mentoring role; the addition of GBL to development of pedagogical activities will enhance the teaching and learning experience. To this end further research could include examination of enthusiasm and emotional engagement in teaching and learning in ICT.

分析：本文的题目是《Play IT：基于游戏的学习方法在编程概念教学中的应用》。文章的"结论"部分的标题是"结论与未来研究范围"（Conclusion and future scope）。可见，在这一部分作者要总结全文并提出未来可以研究的重点。此部分共分为四段，其中第一、二段是对文章研究背景、研究方法、研究过程、研究结果的总结；第三段指出文章的"局限性"，最后一段提出未来可以在哪些方面进行研究。具体分析如下：

第一、二段是文章的"总结"，大意为：本研究以攻读计算机文凭课程的学生为研究对象。我们将基于游戏的策略应用于一组事先没有编程知识的学生,而另一组是最近完成了编程模块的学生。研究结果表明,无论是在科目被教授之前还是在被教授之后,基于游戏的学习都是一种有用的学习策略,但应用在科目被教授之后更有利些。这一研究表明,学生可以利用游戏步骤积极地进行编程的学习。参与学习的 16 名学生认为,游戏学习方法可以使课堂环境变得更有趣,同时也是掌握一些困难概念的有效途径。将游戏元素融入传统教学实践将使学生更主动地参与学习过程。这对教师和学生都是有益的,因为游戏可以让学生在更愉快的学习环境中快速掌握知识。这项研究对目前的教学方法做了有益的补充。

第三段介绍了当前研究的缺陷,大意为:本研究有几个局限:第一,我们无法准确地判断游戏化学习对成功程度、社会互动和自我评估等其他变量的影响;第二,本实验只针对了一个入门课程,而高级编程的教学可能需要一个更复杂的游戏。第三,最后一份问卷调查的应答率很低。

论文 2(Liew & Tan,2016)

题目:The effects of positive and negative mood on cognition and motivation in multimedia learning environment

结论:

Conclusion

Our study generally showed that positive mood had a facilitation effect on cognition and motivation in a multimedia learning system, whereas negative mood had a detrimental effect on multimedia learning. These findings demonstrated that positive mood is desirable for learning in multimedia learning systems, while the presence of negative mood should be mitigated. How can multimedia learning be designed to promote positive mood and to reduce negative mood? One approach is to focus on the visceral design of the multimedia learning interface to induce positive mood. There is a recent research trend that posits emotional design and aesthetic factors, such as colors, anthropomorphism, layouts, and illustrations in multimedia learning systems (Heidig, 2015; Plass et al., 2014; Um et al., 2012).

Yet another approach is to design emotionally intelligent systems that interpret learners' mood profile and provides appropriate feedback as part of a mood regulation strategy (see Sottilare & Proctor, 2012). There is also a huge potential for embodied emotional agents to provide social and emotional support necessary for mood corrections in multimedia learning systems. To conclude, we highlight the need for future works to further explore the relationship among mood, cognition, motivation, and emotion-adaptive strategies in multimedia learning environment. For instance, because negative moods are thought to recruit systematic, cautious and deliberate processing patterns when analyzing new data (Gasper, 2003), it would be interesting to determine if negative moods may actually promote cognitive performance in simulation-based systems that require experimentation, hypotheses testing and discovery-based learning (Liew et al., 2014). In addition, research on how virtual agents and interfaces can be designed to regulate learners' moods in learning systems warrants further attention.

分析：本文题目是《多媒体学习环境中积极情绪和消极情绪对认知和动机的影响》。本文的"结论"部分很简短，只有两个段落。第一段前面两句简单介绍了当前论文的研究结果，后面的句子及整个第二段都是围绕未来的研究方向进行写作。这两段大意为：本研究表明，在多媒体学习系统中，积极情绪对认知和动机有促进作用，而消极情绪对多媒体学习有不利影响。这些发现表明，在多媒体学习系统中，积极的情绪是我们需要的，而消极情绪的存在应该被减少。如何设计多媒体学习来促进积极情绪，减少消极情绪呢？一种方法是侧重于多媒体学习界面的设计，以诱导积极的情绪。最近，有一种研究趋势认为多媒体学习系统可以关注情感设计和审美因素，如色彩、拟人化、布局和插图等。另一种方法是设计情感智能系统，作为情绪调节策略的一部分来解释学习者的情绪状况，并提供适当的反馈。在多媒体学习系统中，具体的情绪代理（emotional agents）有巨大的潜能来提供必要的社会和情感支持来纠正情绪。最后，本文强调今后的研究工作需要进一步探讨多媒体学习环境中情绪、认知、动机和情绪适应策略之间的关系。

综合上面两篇论文的"结论"部分，我们可以看出虽然不同的论文在具体写法上有所差别，但是都围绕着"当前论文的研究结果""未来研究方向或重点"和"当前研究的缺陷"这些方面写作的。

2.11 SSCI 论文整体解析实例

在以上部分，我们对论文各章的写作分别做了分析，下面我们以两篇完整的论文为例来分析论文的写作情况。

论文 1（Ge，2011）

题目：Exploring e-learners' perceptions of net-based peer-reviewed English writing
分析：这篇论文题目是由 explore 的动名词形式构成，整个题目是一个动名词短语,符合我们之前说的"题目一般用名词性结构"的规则。当然,这里提醒一下,题目除了可以用名词性短语结构,还可以用问句的形式。比如,我们可以将这个题目改成"How do e-learners perceive net-based peer-reviewed English writing?"

摘要(Abstract):

This study aims to investigate the effectiveness of a net-based peer review process for improving Chinese adult e-learners' English writing ability. A class of 36 students participated in thiss tudy, which lasted one school year of two semesters. Participants were divided into three groups according to their English writing abilities at the beginning of the study. They attended regular synchronous classes and took writing assignments home. The feature of this experiment is that their writings were submitted for peers' reviews from another group. At the end of each semester, an online writing contest was organized and all the participants took part in order to examine learning outcomes. A survey at the end of the study was also conducted to obtain students' perceptions of the process. The result of the study shows that all the participants obtained satisfactory results, but the students with lower writing ability made more progress than those with higher ability. The finding also indicates that students with higher writing ability tend to become discouraged if they are grouped with lower-ability students for too long.

分析:这个摘要并没有介绍研究背景,而是直接以研究目的开头,本文的研究目的是:探讨基于网络的同行评议过程对提高中国成人网络学习者英语写作能力的有效性。接着,作者介绍了教学实验的情况。实验大致情况如下:实验持续了两个学期(一个学年),有36名参与者,他们在学期初就被按英语写作能力分成了三个小组。参与者参加正常的实时课程,进行课后写作练习。每一组参与者的作文将会提交给其他组的学生进行评价。每个学期,参与者都会进行在线作文测试,以此来检验学习效果。研究结束时的调查问卷收集了参与者对于这一学习过程的感受。最后,摘要介绍了研究结论:所有的参与者都取得了满意的学习效果,但是写作水平较低的学生要比写作水平较高的学生的进步更大。研究暗示,如果高写作水平的学生长时间和低写作水平的学生进行小组合作学习,他们可能会士气低落。

这篇论文的摘要覆盖了摘要的研究目的、研究方法和研究结果三个要点,这三个要点是摘要不可或缺的部分。

关键词(Keywords):Distance education; Peer review; Teaching/learning strategies; Pedagogical issues

分析:一般来说,关键词可以从论文的标题和摘要中获得,但是有必要提醒的是,有的期刊要求关键词只能在其提供的关键词词库里挑选,所以作者在挑选关键词时一定要注意期刊有没有特殊的要求。本文的关键词是在期刊提供的关键词词库中挑选得到的。在挑选时,我们要选择跟文章主题最相关的词语。这里列出的四个关键词比较切合文章主题,如 distance education(远程教育)、peer review(同伴评价)、teaching/learning strategies(教/学策略)、pedagogical issues(教学法话题)。

第一部分:前言(Introduction)

An important goal of teaching English as a foreign language (EFL) is to develop students' writing ability, one of the four skills in language learning, namely listening, speaking, reading and writing. In an e-learning environment, writing classes are often lecture-centered, that is to say, the teacher will spend nearly all the time (normally in an online synchronous class) lecturing about writing skills and evaluating some good or bad writings and then students will be left on their own to do a writing assignment at home and turn in their products online within a specific period of time. But, scholars criticize this teaching method because there is too little exchange between students themselves and students may often feel isolated in learning. Isolation is indeed a common feeling among e-learners. Luckily with the development of the collaborative learning theory since the early 1980s, many e-learning institutions have begun to encourage students to form study groups to facilitate their learning. Many approaches have been done in this field including experimental studies (Suthers and Hundhausen 2003), case analysis (Yukawa 2006), and blended methods (Dwyer and Suthers 2006).

The collaborative learning theory has exerted great influence on language teaching, in which the teaching of writing has been taken as an important experimental field. Many approaches have been developed to encourage students' cooperation and interaction. For example, the Writing Group approach is often adopted to teach writing to undergraduate students. In this approach, students will work in small groups throughout the whole process of writing. They can formulate ideas together and exchange their written drafts and get feedback. The whole process can be very challenging, because every group member needs to be responsible not only for his or her own writing but also for others' (Smith and MacGregor 1992). Another approach called the Writing Fellows was adopted by Tori Haring-Smith in teaching an undergraduate class. These writing fellows were excellent writers chosen from the students and they would be deployed to different classes and read and make comments on the papers of other students (ibid.).

A common goal of these various approaches is to enable students to obtain feedback from each other and then revise and improve their writings based on the feedback. Although scholars have discussed both advantages and disadvantages of peer feedback (see Zamel 1982; Leki 1990; Mendonça and Johnson 1994; Amores 1997; Liu 1998), peer feedback is always deemed as an important and necessary source for learning besides instructor feedback (Villamil and de Guerrero 1998; Yang et al. 2006).

Scholars also believe that peer cooperation and interaction can also facilitate students' writing abilities in an e-learning environment. For example, Warschauer (2002) argued that peer response could promote e-learners' motivation and participation. Hewett (2000) and Tuzi (2004) claimed that peer responses could enable e-learners to revise writings by frequently using ideas from their peers.

Teaching writing by encouraging cooperation and interaction among students is not a new idea in China, but this is still mainly done in traditional face-to-face classes. This study aims to examine the effect of peer cooperation and interaction on students' writing performances in China's online education environment. This may shed some light on the practice.

分析：前言一共分为五段，其中前四段都是对研究背景的介绍，而最后一段则引出当前研究的目的。第一段介绍了时下通常的网络教学中写作教学的基本样式，即以教师的讲座为中心，而学生之间很难有合作和交互。同时，作者指出远程教育机构已经注意到这种教学模式的不足，从而基于合作学习理论（collaborative learning theory）让学生形成学习小组来进行学习。第二段介绍了一些采用了合作式学习小组进行写作教学的实验。第三段指出这些实验的目的就是使学生能够多交互，从而在写作学习中互相促进。第四段指出合作式学习也可以被应用于网络学习环境。最后一段则指出当前研究的目的就是检验中国网络教育情境中的同伴合作和交互对学生写作成绩的影响。

第二部分：文献回顾（Literature review）

Peer collaboration

Proponents of peer collaboration claim that students can learn more of a subject matter, no matter what it is, and retain it longer. Good learning is collaborative but not isolated (Chickering and Gamson 1987; Beckman 1990). Panitz (1997) has listed 67 benefits of collaborative learning, such as building one's self-esteem and establishing peer relationships, etc.

Debates still go on as to the composition of collaborative groups. More and more researchers support diversity in groups with the hope that stronger students can help weaker ones and will benefit from the experience of tutoring (Webb et al. 1998; Dembo and McAuliffe 1987; Hooper and Hannafin 1998). They also found that high-ability students will perform equally well whether in heterogeneous groups or in homogeneous groups. But Mills and Durden (1992) suggested that gifted students might be hindered when they were grouped with weaker students. Radencich and Mckay (1995) also summarized that grouping students according to their ability did not usually benefit overall achievement and they advocated a flexible grouping idea by using a variety of grouping formats. Scholars also debated on the most effective size for groups. For example, Antil et al. (1998) concluded that most teachers who used cooperative learning would use pairs and small groups of three or four at least 57% of the time. Slavin (1987) also showed that groups with two or three members usually would do better than groups with four or more members.

On the other hand, many researchers have pointed out disadvantages of collaborative learning. Salomon (1992) once said that despite the advantages attached to collaborative learning, teams frequently did not work as well as expected. Problems such as the "free rider" effect (Kerr and Brunn 1983) and "ganging up on the task" phenomenon (Salomon and Globerson 1989) often come up in collaborative learning.

Peer review in writing teaching

One form of peer collaboration in practicing writing is peer review. Peer review, sometimes named as peer assessment or peer editing, usually means that students check each other's drafts and then provide feedback to each other. A more detailed definition of peer review is provided by Liu and Hansen (2002) who argued that it was the use of learners instead of a teacher as sources of information and interaction in commenting on each other's drafts in the process of writing.

Many scholars have stated that the usefulness and effectiveness of a peer review process in improving learners' writing abilities can make students more actively involved in the writing process instead of passively receiving information from the teacher (Mittan 1989) and that students can reflect on their own writings in light of their peers' comments (Mendonça and Johnson 1994), enabling students to build up critical skills needed to analyze and revise their own writings (Leki 1990). Chaulk (1994) claimed that teachers' feedback was often rather general, while responses from students could be more specific. He reported that his students could and did revise effectively based on comments from their peers. Villamil and de Guerrero (1998) in their investigation of peer revision on students' final drafts found that peer feedback could develop students' potential for effective revision. Tsui and Ng (2000), through their work, claimed that peer comments could contribute positively to secondary L2 (second language) writers' writing process. They pointed out that peer comments could make students more aware of their own strengths and weaknesses and encourage more cooperation among them.

The peer review practice also finds its way in China's EFL teaching environment. Xu (2000) concluded from a questionnaire survey among 58 college students that most students held a positive attitude towards peer assessment. Zhang (2008) also claimed that peer feedback could be a necessary complement to teacher feedback in practicing writing.

While the usefulness of peer review has been admitted in writing teaching, scholars have also pointed out some shortcomings and uncertainties of this practice. Zhang (1995) suggested that students participating in the peer review process might sometimes doubt the correctness and accuracy of the comments from peers, and they also tended to be overly critical of each other's writings. Amores (1997) also indicated that some students might resent acting like a teacher and became uneasy in editing peers' writings. Saito and Fujita (2004) suggested that friendship bias, reference bias, purpose bias, collusive bias and feedback bias might appear in some cases. Research has also shown that students favored teacher feedback rather than peer feedback.

Yang et al. (2006), after analyzing some textual and questionnaire data, concluded that although peer feedback could facilitate students' writing practice, teacher feedback was more likely to be adopted by students to improve their writing. This conclusion is echoed by some other researchers like Qi (2004). Some research indicates that students sometimes have negative reactions to peer response (Fei 2006).

While the above research is all about the use of peer review in a face-to-face teaching environment, scholars also admit the feasibility of applying the practice in an e-learning environment. Research has been done to explore issues like the effectiveness of synchronous online peer responses and revisions (Hansen and Liu 2005). Online peer response is believed to promote student motivation, participation, and collaboration (Warschauer 2002), and facilitate students' revisions of their writings (Tuzi 2004).

分析：该文的文献回顾划分为两个小节，分别是"同伴合作"（Peer collaboration）和"写作教学中的同伴评价"（Peer review in writing teaching）。

"同伴合作"一节分为三段。第一段指出协作学习的好处。第二段指出学术界对于合作学习小组的构成存在争论，有的学者认为同质化小组（homogeneous groups）好，有的人则认为异质化小组（heterogeneous groups）好。第三段指出，有的学者认为合作学习也可能会带来一些负面效应，如"搭便车效应"（free rider effect）和"联合起来完成任务"的现象（ganging up on the task phenomenon）。

"写作教学中的同伴评价"一节分为五段。第一段指出写作训练的一种同伴合作形式就是同伴评价。第二段介绍了同伴评价的优点。第三段介绍了同伴评价在中国英语教学中的应用。第四段则指出同伴评价中可能存在的缺点。第五段指出前人的此类研究多是在传统的面授课堂中进行的，但其实此类方法也可以在网络教学情境中进行。

第三部分：研究问题（Research questions）

In research about face-to-face writing teaching, students usually knew who they were collaborating with. The familiarity might have led to some unwanted effects; for example, students might feel uneasy in commenting on their friends' writings. In the Chinese culture, people tend to avoid finding fault with each other so as to save face. So what if peer review activities are blind?

In the above mentioned online writing teaching research, the peer review activities usually were carried out synchronously, that is to say, students needed to meet online at the same time. But as e-learners in China are mostly full-time job holders, this time requirement may be unsuitable. Recently many e-learning institutions in mainland China have begun to advocate asynchronous learning in teaching their students. Synchronous communication between students and between students and their instructors has become less and less. This change may imply that we should make more efforts to facilitate asynchronous collaboration among students.

The investigation presented in this study aimed to test the feasibility and effectiveness of applying the peer review practice to the teaching of English writing in an e-learning environment. The peer review activities described here are blind and asynchronous in nature. Participants were divided into different groups and would practice their English writing through a peer review process, which is a form of collaborative learning.

The researcher expected that all the participants would improve their

English writing abilities after this two-semester-long experiment. Participants' perceptions of the collaborative experience were also obtained. Therefore, a survey was conducted at the end of the investigation to address the following questions:

(1) Did all the participants improve their English writing, and which group improved most?

(2) What did they benefit most from the peer review process?

(3) Is it necessary for the instructor to provide guidance or consulting in the peer review process?

分析：这一部分共分为四段。第一段指出同伴互评的一个可能的缺陷就是"同伴之间可能互相认识，从而对互评的结果造成影响"。作者顺势引出盲审（blind peer review）可能可以克服这一缺陷。第二段指出，同步的（synchronous）同伴互评有不方便之处，从而引入异步的（asynchronous）同伴互评。第三段简要介绍了当前研究的实验构想，即采用异步的同伴互评。第四段介绍了当前研究的三个具体研究问题：1)所有参与者都提高了写作成绩吗？哪一组提高的最多？2)参与者在同伴互评的过程中最受益的是什么？3)教师需不需要在同伴互评的过程中提供指导？

第四部分：研究方法（Method）

Participants

A class of 36 students majoring in Telecommunications Engineering from the School of Network Education at Beijing University of Posts and Telecommunications participated in the study. Consent was obtained from the school and all the participants. They took part in an online English writing quiz at the beginning of the study (this quiz, the home assignments for students to do in the study and the two writing contests at the end of the two semesters had the same requirements and were marked by the same course instructor according to the same set of rules, which are shown in Appendix A), and they were divided into three groups based on their scores (see Table 1).

Table 1　Grouping based on students' writing scores

Group	total number of students	range of scores	mean of scores
A	8	score>75	78
B	11	60< score ⩽ 75	64
C	17	score ⩽ 60	43

Group A was designated as the upper level; Group B, the intermediate level, and Group C, the lower level. Group A consisted of 8 students; Group B, 11; and Group C, 17. As some research has indicated that grouping students according to ability may make low-achievers feel upset and communicate self-fulfilling low expectations (Slavin 1987; Hooper and Hannafin 1998), the instructor did not tell the students about which group they belonged to with the hope to avoid this unwanted effect. They had the same instructor and they used the same materials. Students' email addresses were collected for use in the study.

The scores were then processed for a descriptive analysis with the use of SPSS. From Table 2, we can see the standard deviations of Group A and B are small but that of Group C is rather large. This shows that the students of Group C were very different in their writing abilities. The mean differences among the three groups are large, too and this shows that the three groups were very different in their overall writing abilities.

Table 2 Descriptive analysis of the quiz scores

group	Number	Mean	Minimum	Maximum	Std. Deviation
Group A	8	78.0000	76.00	81.00	2.13809
Group B	11	64.0000	61.00	72.00	3.25576
Group C	17	43.0000	28.00	57.00	7.81825
Total	36	57.1944	28.00	81.00	15.59637

The quiz scores were put to a nonparametric test to see whether the differences were statistically significant. Table 3 shows that there were statistically significant differences among the three groups.

Table 3 Kruskal-Wallis Test Statistics[a,b] of the quiz

	Group	N	Mean Chi-Square	Rank	df	Asymp. Sig.
quiz	Group A	8	32.50			
	Group B	11	23.00			
	Group C	17	9.00			
	Total	36	30.021		2	0.000

Note: a. Kruskal Wallis Test
  b. Grouping Variable: group

Procedure

There would be one synchronous learning class every other week in the two semesters (about 8 months). Each class lasted about 3 h with two intervals. The classes were recorded simultaneously by a web tool named Webex (http://www.webex.com.cn) and uploaded to the online forum of the course. All the students were required to take part in the classes or watch the recordings; otherwise they would not even know what topic they should write on. Since the number of students was very large and online synchronous discussions among students were hard to control, the classes were lecture-centered with occasional discussions between students and the instructor. In the first synchronous class, the instructor explained to the students about the workflow of the peer review process (but not tell them about which group they belonged to or would work with), but there would be no requirements about how to comment on a peer's writings, that is to say, the students were left on their own to make judgments on each other's writings. In each synchronous class, the students were assigned a writing homework (so in sum, the students would do 16 home writing assignments) and were required to submit their writings through e-mail to the instructor in 2 days (Phase one). The assignment was usually a short passage of at least 150 words on a certain topic. The instructor would examine the writings first to check their originality. If he detected any plagiarism in one's paper, the student would be excluded from the study. If not, the instructor sent the student's writing to one peer in another group for peer reviewing (Phase two). The peer review process was conducted rotationally; for example, this time it was Group A working with Group B, but the next time it was Group A with Group C, and so on. Students in Group B and C also underwent the same process. Students completed the review process in 2 days and sent the commented writings to the instructor again (Phase three). This requirement was to ensure that the peer review process was a blind one so that the side effects mentioned in the part of "the Present Study" would not appear. The instructor then sent the commented writings to their original writers (Phase four). Figure 1 shows the workflow of the peer review process. The dotted line connecting the instructor and Student C means Student C was not in the present round, but in the next.

As can be seen from the description above, each time the student interacted indirectly through the instructor with a peer from a different group. This indirect interaction like direct interaction could also enable them to know each other's writing abilities and each other's opinions on their own writings. This design was to ensure the student to have access to writings of different levels, as some researchers have shown that students will perform better when working in heterogeneous groups (Slavin 1987; Hooper and Hannafin 1998).

During the whole peer review process, the instructor mainly acted as a messenger for the peers, but in the online synchronous class following each assignment, the instructor spent some time summarizing students' performance in their writings and pointing out problems in the review process. These advices and suggestions were to help improve students' performance in the next peer review round. So the instructor also played the role of facilitator or supervisor in the study.

An online writing contest was organized to evaluate their learning outcomes at the end of each semester. The contests were actually quizzes like the one at the beginning of the study but were given the name "contest" to make them appear more formal and conclusive. All students were required to take part in the contests, and if not they would be excluded from the study. The contests had the same requirements as the home assignments. This was to make students' improvement in writing easily detected. Students submitted their writings for the contests through e-mail to the teacher in 2 days. An e-mail survey was conducted at the end of the second semester to investigate participants' perceptions of the peer review process (see Appendix B).

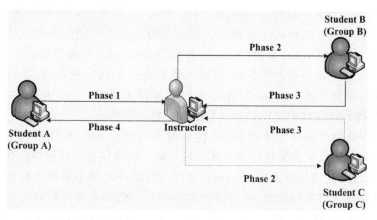

Fig. 1 Workflow of the peer review process

分析:研究方法这一章分为两个小节,分别是"参与者"(Participants)和"实验步骤"(Procedure)。

"参与者"一节分为四段。第一段介绍了参与者的情况:参与者是北京一所网络教育机构的36名学生,全部来自同一个班级。在实验开始前,对参与者进行了一次在线英语写作前测,根据测验的结果(如该文 Table 1 所示)将参与者分成了三组。前测、家庭作业和实验过程中使用的两次后测均有相同的要求,测验的评分由同一名教师完成,评分标准见该文的附录 A(Appendix A)。第二段介绍了分组情况:Group A 被定为高级别小组,包含 8 名学生;Group B 是中级别小组,有 11 名学生;Group C 是低级别小组,有 17 名学生。研究者并没有告诉参与者们被分在了哪一个小组,这是为了避免一些水平较低的学生受到打击。各小组的授课教师和教材都相同。第三段介绍了前测的情况:根据该文 Table 2,Group A 和 Group B 的前测成绩标准差很小,而 Group C 的标准差则很大;此外,三个小组的平均分差别较大。第四段指出,前测成绩进行了非参数检验(nonparametric test),该文的 Table 3 显示三个小组的前测成绩有显著差异。

"实验步骤"一节分为四段。第一段详细介绍了实验进行的过程:实验持续 2 个学期,共 8 个月。每隔一周会安排一次同步网络授课(Synchronous Class),授课全程使用网络工具 Webex 录制,每次授课会布置一次家庭写作练习(共 16 次)。所有参与者必须参加网络授课或者观看授课录像,否则他们根本不知道家庭作业的话题。考虑到班级人数较多,网络授课还是以教师讲座为中心,辅以少量的讨论活动。在第一次网络授课中,教师会告知学生同伴互评的流程(但是不告知学生他们被分进了哪个小组)。实验并不对具体的同伴评价做要求,学生可以根据自己的判断对同伴的写作作业进行评价。同伴互评的流程如该文的 Fig.1 所示:阶段 1,学生需要在 2 天内通过 E-mail 将作业(作业基本都是针对一个话题写一篇 150 字左右的短文)结果发给教师。然后,教师会浏览作业,检查作业有无抄袭,如果发现抄袭,该名参与者将会被排除在实验之外。阶段 2,如果作业没有抄袭,教师会通过 E-mail 将该作业发送给一名来自其他小组的学生进行同伴评价。同伴评价将循环进行,如这次 Group A 和 Group B 合作,下次 Group A 和 Group C 合作,以此类推。阶段 3,收到同伴的作业后,评价人需要在 2 天内完成评价,并将结果通过 E-mail 发给教师。可以看出,同伴之间并不能直接接触,从而达到匿名的效果。阶段 4,教师再将收到的评价结果反馈给作业的原作者。

第二段介绍了同伴互评在不同小组间循环进行的目的,即让不同小组的学生能够接触到不同水平的写作结果。第三段介绍了教师在这一过程中的作用。作者提到,教师主要起到传话人(Messenger)的作用,但是在网络课堂上教师也会对上一次的同伴评价结果做梳理,从而帮助学生在下一轮同伴互评中能得到提高。从这一意义上来讲,教师承担了"促进者"(Facilitator)和"监督者"(Supervisor)的角色。第四段介绍,每个学期末都会安排一次在线后测,后测形式和前测、家庭作业一样。所有的参与者必须完成后测,否则就被排除在实验之外。在第 2 个学期末研究者还进行了一次电子邮件问卷调查,以此来获取参与者对于学习过程的感知数据。

从以上分析我们可以看出,在"研究方法"这一章,该文对实验的过程有着非常详尽的描述,这也是一篇合格论文所必须做到的。

第五部分:结果和讨论(Results and discussion)(注:有的文章将结果和讨论分

成两章)

The peer review process required every reviewer to be responsible for others' writings. They might point out the vocabulary or structural errors of their peers' works, and they could also see others' comments on their own writings. But the collaboration between them employed a new form in the experiment. Traditional forms of collaboration include peer teaching, peer learning, study groups and so on, which were classified by Davis (1993) into three general types: informal learning groups, formal learning groups, and study teams. Whatever the name is, most of them tend to focus on collaboration between students themselves. The collaboration described in this study was via the instructor, who served as a messenger and supervisor. The teacher's participation as described in the above section might have reinforced students' collaboration and made the whole process proceed in the right direction. Another feature of the collaboration is that the students did not have a stable collaborative relationship. They might have a different partner to work with each time. This changing nature of collaboration was interesting and challenging to them. What's more, they did not know the names of their partners, so their collaborative relationship was a blind one.

After the first contest at the end of the first semester, students' scores were processed for a descriptive analysis and a nonparametric test (see Tables 4 and 5).

Table 4 Descriptive analysis of Contest 1

group	Number	Mean	Minimum	Maximum	Std. Deviation
Group A	8	80.0000	77.00	84.00	2.56348
Group B	11	69.0000	61.00	78.00	7.52330
Group C	17	46.0000	31.00	62.00	8.41873
Total	36	60.5833	31.00	84.00	16.17472

Table 5 Kruskal-Wallis Test Statistics[a,b] of Contest 1

	Group	N	Mean Rank	Chi-Square	df	Asymp. Sig.
quiz	Group A	8	31.94			
	Group B	11	23.18			
	Group C	17	9.15			
	Total	36		28.698	2	0.000

Note: a. Kruskal Wallis Test
b. Grouping Variable: group

Compared with Table 2, Table 4 shows that the means for the three groups had increased, which implies that the overall writing abilities of all the groups had improved. While the standard deviations of Group A and C remained almost unchanged, that of Group B became very large. This change indicates that the differences within Group B were more dispersed than before. The nonparametric test shows that the differences among the three groups were still significant.

It was also found that students in Group A were still the best writers among all the groups, but Group B improved more greatly. Students from Group C also improved but not that much. Five students from Group B met the standard of Group A and two students from Group C reached the requirement for Group B. Table 6 and Fig. 2 shows the results.

Table 6 Overview of Contest 1

Group	total number of students	range of scores	mean of scores
A	8	score>75	80
B	11	60<score≤75(6 students)	69
		score>75(5 students)	
C	17	score≤60(15 students)	46
		60<score≤75(2 students)	

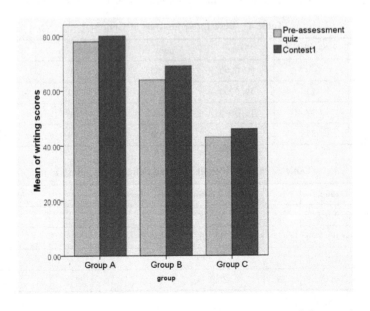

Fig. 2 Comparison between the pre-assessment quiz and Contest 1

After the second contest at the end of the second semester, results changed. Students from Group C improved most. Group B still progressed but not as much as in the first semester. Students in Group A, on the other hand, improved less than the other two groups throughout the two semesters, although they were still the best writers among the groups. Eight students from Group C now met the standard of Group B as is shown in Table 7 and Fig. 3.

Table 7　Overview of Contest 2

Group	total number of students	range of scores	mean of scores
A	8	score＞75	82
B	11	60＜score≤75(6 students)	71
		score＞75 (5 students)	
C	17	score≤60(9 students)	61
		60＜score≤75(8 students)	

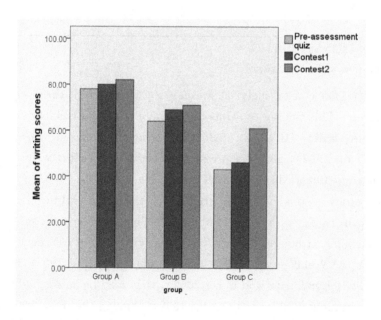

Fig. 3　Comparison between the pre-assessment quiz and the two contests

The scores were also processed for a descriptive analysis and a nonparametric test. Table 8 shows that the means of the three groups increased again, with that of Group C significantly increased 61 ð Þ 46 1/4 15 . The standard deviations of Group B and C were still very large, which implies that the students in these two groups were still very uneven in their writing abilities. The nonparametric test shows that the differences among the three groups were significant (Table 9).

Table 8 Descriptive analysis of Contest 2

group	Number	Mean	Minimum	Maximum	Std. Deviation
Group A	8	82.0000	76.00	87.00	3.46410
Group B	11	71.0000	62.00	82.00	7.65506
Group C	17	61.0000	40.00	75.00	9.08295
Total	36	68.7222	40.00	87.00	11.30262

Table 9 Kruskal-Wallis Test Statistics[a,b] of Contest 2

	Group	N	Mean Chi-Square	Rank	df	Asymp. Sig.
quiz	Group A	8	31.38			
	Group B	11	20.86			
	Group C	17	10.91			
	Total	36				
			21.366		2	0.000

Note: a. Kruskal Wallis Test
b. Grouping Variable: group

From the above data analysis, we can see that all the three groups made some progress. This finding confirms the common idea that collaborative learning can be very rewarding (Beckman 1990; Chickering and Gamson 1987; Johnson et al. 1991; Panitz 1997), and peer review is effective in teaching writing (Villamil and de Guerrero 1998; Zhang 2008; Tsui and Ng 2000; Xu 2000). On the other hand, the study also shows that students with lower abilities made greater progress than those with higher abilities. This finding is consistent with observations that although high-ability students can perform equally well in various groups (Webb et al. 1998; Dembo and McAuliffe 1987; Hooper and Hannafin 1998; Lundstrom and Baker 2009), they may be held up when grouped with weaker students (Mills and Durden 1992). Among the three groups, Group C was the weakest, but when they worked with Group A and B, they made the greatest progress in the long run. This finding also confirms the idea that for those less mature EFL writers, peer comments lead to positive results (Tsui and Ng 2000). On the other hand, Group A was the strongest but their writing abilities did not seem to improve much. Some students in Group A stated in the survey that comments from others provided little help for them, so they did not make any revisions of their original writings. Table 10 also shows that no one in Group A revised their writings. As practice makes perfect, this attitude might have hindered their improvement in writing.

All the participants responded to the survey conducted at the end of the second semester. They all held a positive attitude towards the peer review experience. But when asked if it was necessary to prolong the experiment, both Group B and C said "Yes", while only three from Group A thought so. The other five participants from Group A stated in their answers to the open question in the survey (see examples in Appendix C) that they put too much effort in the peer review process but received too little, and they felt that they had been taken advantage of by the school. This implies that these students could resent the peer review process if they were always helping out students, but not getting much help back. This finding indicates that the participants with lower writing abilities were better motivated and those with higher abilities might have high interest in the beginning but tend to be under-motivated and even bored if they continued working with those with lower abilities. This finding is consistent with that of Mills and Durden (1992). Flexible grouping may be more suitable for them in the long run (Radencich and Mckay 1995). Besides, some students from Group A and B thought some comments from their peers were not right or reasonable (see Appendix C), and this finding echoes conclusions from some other scholars (Nelson and Murphy 1992; Zhang 1995).

All groups thought they still needed synchronous classes. In their mind, synchronous learning could provide them with basic writing skills from the instructor and they thought this was essential for their study. They stated that they seemed unable to concentrate on the learning process without this. This finding is consistent with previous observations that asynchronous and synchronous e-learning can complement each other and the combination of these two types of e-learning supports several ways for learners and teachers to exchange information, collaborate on work, and get to know each other (Haythornthwaite and Kazmer 2002). As indicated by some scholars, asynchronous learning can provide students with more autonomy, allow students to be free from the constraints of time and space (Kruse 2004), and thus improve one's personal ability in self-study (Robert and Dennis 2005), while synchronous learning is essential to SLA (second language acquisition), and it can duplicate some elements of the traditional face-to-face classes, enable students to receive immediate feedback from other learners and the teacher (Keegan et al. 2005), and thus involve more interaction between teachers and students or among students (Pfister 2005). In the case of this study, although students did not know who they were collaborating with, they still got to know each other's opinions on their writing.

All the students thought it was very interesting and challenging to comment on others' writings. Students in Group A stated that they enjoyed finding errors and mistakes in others' compositions, especially those badly written, and they did not hesitate in commenting on these mistakes. They often felt proud that their own writings were better than those they commented on. Students in Group C said that they were very cautious in the peer review process. They thought they could tell that they were being critiqued by someone who knew more than they did and could articulate it better in English, and so were afraid to make any wrong comment on others' work. They would often use dictionaries or resources on the Internet to help themselves. They thought they might have benefited much from this "cautiousness". On the other hand, they often felt inferior in the writing ability to their peers from other groups. Four of them stated in the survey that they had become less confident in English writing and five others said they were determined to catch up with those highability students. This implies that the heterogeneous grouping may have different impacts on low-ability students: Some may be encouraged while others may be discouraged. Students in Group B often had mixed feelings. They did not necessarily know the group structure of the experiment, but they could tell when their paper was being critiqued by a student whose English was better or worse than theirs, so they would feel superior when reviewing writings worse than theirs but inferior when reading works better than theirs. Anyway, they knew they were still not so good at writing, so they would not stop practicing. In other words, all the groups were willing to assume responsibility. This finding confirms Johnson and Johnson's (2004) belief that individual accountability is one of the five basic elements needed for effective group collaboration. Some scholars even claim individual accountability to be the most critical factor in collaborative learning, and a lack of it can impede collaboration (An et al. 2008). The positive attitude of the students towards peer review is also consistent with previous research findings that most students will favor the peer review practice in writing and peer cooperation is a good complement to teachers' instruction (Xu 2000; Yang et al.

2006).

Interestingly, all the participants focused their attention on grammatical mistakes in others' writings, with students in Group A occasionally commenting on others' wording or textual organization. This phenomenon was also found in some other research (see Zhang 2008). The reason may be that most adult e-learners in China are poor in English and that most tests for e-learners of non-English majors in China still focus on students' grammatical and vocabulary abilities. This special focus on grammar and vocabulary might account for the most prominent progress in Group B and C. They could use more grammatical structures and more varied vocabularies in writing. For example, they would sometimes use "affection" instead of "love".

When asked whether they rewrote on the topics after obtaining others' comments, 13 Students in Group C said they rewrote on all or some of the topics, and five students in Group B did so, but none in Group A. This shows that most low-ability students had made good use of peer feedback, but most of those with intermediate or high writing abilities did not. Students in Group A stated that their writings were almost always commented favorably by others, so they thought they didn't need to rewrite.

All the participants stated that although they appreciated the comments from their peers, they still wanted to know the teacher's opinions. They thought comments from the teacher would be more appropriate. In other words, theses students still believed in the authority of their teacher (Tsui and Ng 2000; Lee 2004; Lee 2008), and the teacher's feedback, if there was any, was more likely to be adopted (Qi 2004; Yang et al. 2006; Zhang 2008; Zhao 2010). From another perspective, this may mean that students sometimes lack trust in peer feedback (Zhang 1995). This finding echoes the idea that the teacher needs to act as both a facilitator and authority in the classroom (O'Dwyer 2006).

As to the online writing contests, all the students in Group A requested more, but only a few from Group B and C held the same idea. This may lies in the fact that the students in Group A had more confidence in their writing ability and they wanted opportunities to show that they were better than others.

分析：第一段简要回顾了实验的特色：该实验采用了匿名同伴互评的方式，而且每一轮同伴互评的对象都来自不同级别的小组。

第二、三、四段介绍了第 1 个学期末举行的第 1 次后测的情况。和该文的 Table 2 比起来，Table 4 显示三个小组的平均分都有提高，Group A 和 Group C

的标准差几乎没变,而 Group B 的标准差变得很大。这一变化表明 Group B 的组内差异比以前更加分散了。该文的 Table 5 显示,三个小组的组间差异仍然显著。同时,在这一阶段,Group A 仍然是三个小组中成绩最好的,而 Group B 则提高得更快,Group C 虽然也有提高,但是幅度不大。Group B 中有 5 名学生的成绩达到了 Group A 的程度,而 Group C 中有 2 名学生的成绩达到了 Group B 的程度(参考该文的 Table 6 和 Fig. 2)。

第五段和第六段介绍了第 2 个学期末的后测情况。结果显示,Group C 的成绩提高最多,Group B 也有进步,但是提高幅度没有第 1 次后测大了。Group A 的学生在两次后测中的提高幅度比其他两组都要小,但是该组仍是成绩最好的。在这一阶段,Group C 中有 8 名学生达到了 Group B 的程度(参考该文的 Table 7 和 Fig. 2)。表 8 显示,第 2 次后测中,三个小组的平均分再次得到提高,Group C 提高的幅度最大。Group B 和 Group C 的标准差仍然很大。表 9 显示三个小组的组间差异仍然显著。

第七段,文章对上面几段的数据结果进行了讨论。文章认为,上文的结果证实了一个普遍的观点,即合作式学习可以取得良好的学习效果,并且同伴互评在写作教学中是有效的。同时,研究结果还表明低水平的参与者会比高水平的参与者在同伴互评的过程中得到更大的提高,而高水平学生和低水平学生合作时,高水平学生会受到一定的阻碍。

这一部分的剩余段落介绍了问卷调查的结果,并进行了讨论。大意为:首先,所有的参与者对于这一同伴互评的学习过程都是持正面意见的。但是,在被问到"是否愿意继续进行这种学习方式"时,Group A 中只有两名学生选择了"是",而其他两组则全部选择了肯定的回答。Group A 中选择"否"的学生给出的原因是:他们在同伴互评中付出太多,而收获太少,他们似乎被学校"利用"了。这一发现表明高水平的学生在这一学习过程中的学习动机被削弱了。其次,三个小组的参与者都认为同步网络授课是必须的,因为这种授课可以让他们从教师那里得到直接的指导,完全自主式的学习方式似乎并不适合他们。再次,所有的学生都认为对同伴的作业进行评价是有趣且有挑战性的。同时,研究还发现所有的学生在进行同伴评价时,过于关注语法错误,只有 Group A 的学生偶尔关注了词汇和句子结构等问题。这一现象可能与这些网络成人学生较低的英语水平有关。最后,所有的参与者都认为,他们仍然希望教师能给自己的作业进行评价,也就是说,这些学生仍然认为教师具有权威性。

从上面文章的写作中可以看出,在结果和讨论部分,我们不仅需要对文章的实验数据进行完整地呈现,还需要对结果反映出的问题做出分析,同时还要将当前研究的发现和前人的研究发现进行对比,从而突出当前研究的创新之处。

第 6 部分：结论（Conclusion）

Online collaborative learning has long been advocated by educators. But they often debate on the specific formats to be taken. In the teaching of writing to undergraduate students, many approaches have been developed, such as those mentioned in the Introduction. As more and more e-learning institutions in China are reducing synchronous classes and most synchronous classes are still lecture-centered, there is a special need to find ways to involve all the students in the learning process. The approach in this study was to improve students' English writing skills through a peer review process. The result showed that most participants accepted this approach and received satisfactory results. Students with higher writing abilities enjoyed the process of commenting on others' works, and they built up more confidence in learning. Those with lower abilities might have lost confidence in the Computer-Supported Collaborative Learning process, but they made the greatest progress and they were the most prominent beneficiaries. As to the few who were not satisfied with the process, special care might be given to them. Maybe they needed more challenging tasks to facilitate their learning. This is not so difficult to realize. In any case, e-learners need to experience learning successes that can build their competence, control and worth (Cheng and Lin 2010).

On the other hand, there are some limitations of this study that need to be recognized. First, the sample size of this study is relatively small. The small sample size may not represent the overall situations of adult e-learners in China. Second, it is indicated that the peer review form in this study was more to the advantage of the students with low or intermediate writing abilities, so there was a kind of unfairness for those high-ability students. Are there more appropriate forms of peer review that can facilitate all the participants? Third, the survey indicated that all the students called for the instructor's feedback, but due to various considerations the instructor actually did not give one-to-one feedback in the study. So what results will come up if there is some teacher feedback? All these questions are worthy of consideration and call for further exploration.

分析：作为文章结尾的"结论"部分，写起来并不难。从该文的这一部分我们看出，作者将其分成了二段。第一段对文章的研究结果进行了总结，而第二段则提出了文章的不足之处，并为未来的研究提出建议。这种写法是大多数研究论文所遵循的方法。我们需要注意的是，在对文章进行总结时，行文和摘要要有所区别。摘要也需要对研究结果进行描述，但是更为简洁，而结论部分的总结则需要更全面和具体一些。

论文 2（Hummel，Boyle，Einarsdóttir，Pétursdóttir，& Graur，2018）

（文中的图表和附录较多，这里不提供本文的图表，原文可以在以下地址下载：https://pan.baidu.com/s/1nTAXIBvTp_3TN5bQDqQQmw；提取码：uv5o）

题目（Title）：Game-based career learning support for youth：Effects of playing the Youth@Work game on career adaptability

分析：这一题目直接用了名词短语的形式，冒号前后各是一个名词短语。冒号前面的名词短语中心词是 support（支持），冒号后面的中心词是 effects（效果、影响），这两个中心词前后都有限定成分。这个题目大意为：基于游戏的对青少年职业学习的支持——Youth@Work 游戏对职业适应性的影响。

摘要（Abstract）：

Choosing a career is one of the most important decisions that youth has to take but many young people find this a hard issue to engage with. Current career counselling practice does not appear very compelling or motivating to young people. Professional games could provide a more engaging and motivating way of acquiring professional awareness and competence for career decision making and learning. We present the design and effects of playing a game that aims to increase career awareness and adaptabilities in youth (13-19 years). In a Randomized Controlled Trial，93 high school students from Iceland and Romania were asked to carry out career-oriented activities，with half playing an interactive game and the other half performing a paper-and-pencil version of the same activities. The students were compared on career adaptability, career learning and career awareness scores before and after these interventions. Main results show that engaging players in these career-oriented activities has short term effects on outcome scores for career adaptabilities and for perceptions of career learning competences. Students who played the game report significantly faster growth on career adaptabilities that deal with "concern"，"control" and "confidence". It can therefore be concluded that introducing game-based learning in career decision support for youth is a promising endeavour.

分析：第一，摘要在开头的两句话里介绍了目前青少年职业选择方面的困境，主要是目前的职业咨询方法对年轻人来说不具有吸引力。第二，作者引出本文的话题：职业游戏可以为职业决策和学习提供一个更有吸引力的方法。第三，作者介绍了本文的研究目的：主要是旨在提高青少年（13～19 岁）的职业意识和职业适应力。第四，作者介绍了参与者和实验方法：参与者是 93 名来自冰岛和罗马尼亚的高中生，采用随机对照实验，一半的参与者玩互动游戏，而另一半玩同一游戏的纸笔版，最后比较干预前后学生的职业适应性、职业学习和职业意识得分。第五，作者介绍了实验结果：利用游戏进行职业方面的指导，对于参与者的职业适应性和他们对职业学习能力的感知方面有着短期影响，玩过这款游戏的学生在和"关注""控制""信心"相关的职业适应性上有较大提升。第六，作者指出本文的结论就是：在青少年职业决策的支持方面，引入相关游戏是值得尝试的方向。

这篇论文的摘要同样也覆盖了摘要研究目的、研究方法和研究结果三个点。

关键词（Keywords）：Game design; professional games; career decision making; career awareness; career adaptabilities; career learning; career competence framework; vocational interests

分析：作者给出了 8 个关键词，这算是较多的关键词了，一般给出 3~5 个即可。这 8 个关键词是：游戏设计；职业游戏；职业决策；职业意识；职业适应性；职业学习；职业能力框架；职业兴趣。一般来说，我们可以从论文的标题中选择关键词，这里作者显然并非如此。根据论文题目，其实我们可以将关键词精简为：professional games（职业游戏）、career learning（职业学习）和 career adaptability（职业适应性），这三个关键词足够覆盖本文的话题。

第一部分：前言（Introduction）

Choosing a career is one of the most important decisions a young person has to make, but is also one that many find difficult to relate to adequately and at the appropriate time. Young people's confidence, career aspirations, awareness of possibilities and attitudes towards suitable professions to a large degree determine later career choice and success (Hodkinson & Sparkes, 1997). It is therefore crucial that young people start thinking about professional careers at an early stage and in a both positive and realistic way. Acquiring sufficient career awareness and career decision management skills (like setting targets, planning and taking ownership) can be expected to positively increase career outcomes and reduce the risk of dropping out of school later (Law, 1996; Roberts, 1997; Watts, 2001). For many young people however, current career counselling practice does not appear to be compelling or motivating (Amundson, 2003; Lovén, 2003). We need more engaging and active ways of supporting youth in career decision making, ways that are more aligned with their real life learning.

Games that aim to foster the acquisition of learning objectives are called "serious" to denote that they are not just fun to play, but also hold potential as cognitive tools for learning (e.g. Michael & Chen, 2006; Connolly, Boyle, Hainey, MacArthur, & Boyle, 2012). Game-based learning can be a valuable way to engage students in learning, as it fits well with their daily computer use. Especially in vocational education, motivation and effective acquisition of professional skills have been problematic and in need of improvement (e. g. Van der Veen, Weijers, Dikkers, Hornstra, & Peetsma, 2014). So called "professional" games are increasingly being used as a more motivating and immersive way to have learners experience work challenges and assess them on practice skills for professional life in context (Hummel, Geerts, Slootmaker, Kuipers, & Westera, 2015; Hummel, Nadolski, Eshuis, & Slootmaker, 2016; Hummel, Nadolski, Joosten-ten Brinke, & Baartman, 2017). Review studies have shown that effective game design is key ("garbage in, garbage out") for achieving actual motivation and learning effects in education (Boyle, Hainey, et al., 2016; Clark, Tanner-Smith, & Killingsworth, 2016).

The combination of school and gaming has potential to increase learning, especially for lower performing, disengaged students (Shute, Ventura, Bauer, & Zapata-Rivera, 2009). Playing games in education is generally known for its contribution to improving motoric skills or gaining knowledge about certain school topics. Less known is that serious games also foster the acquisition of more complex and more generic skills, like problem solving and professional competence or awareness (GuillénNieto & Aleson-Carbonell, 2012; Yang, 2012), like is required in career decision making. We will therefore argue and examine the compelling and innovative idea to develop and use a serious professional game to support youth in their career decision making. The use of TEL in career counselling has been rare and existing career games are very scarce (with My Tycoon probably being the most relevant exception). Boyle, Allan, et al. (2016) did identify a few papers about games for careers, going back as far as 1971, but none of these contained high quality experimental evaluations of resources.

Serious games for acquiring professional competence (like career decision making) have been found to offer learning activity that better stimulates intrinsic motivation when compared to more traditional ways of learning (Garris, Ahlers, & Driskell, 2002; Ryan & Deci, 2000; Tsai, Tsai, & Lin, 2015; Wouters & van Oostendorp, 2013). Professional games stand the challenge of being both authentic (realistic) and playful (engaging) at the same time. This implies a design effort that requires close collaboration between content experts (i. e. in career counselling practice), game developers and instructional designers. To warrant authenticity, learning contexts have to resemble contexts where students apply what has been learned. In that way learning becomes motivating and more likely to transfer to real world situations (Herrington, Oliver, & Reeves, 2003). To warrant playful learning, the gameplay has to integrate personalised feedback, support and scoring mechanisms in an unobtrusive way (i.e. embedded in the game narrative). Current approaches for integrating personalised feedback gather data about learners' progress and are technically grounded in learner modelling (Khenissi, Essalmi, & Jemni, 2015). Creating such a learner model requires many observations of learner-game interactions and interpreting these in terms of progress towards learning outcomes. As an example, Shute and colleagues used the framework of Evidence Centered Design (ECD) to develop conceptual assessment models, which in turn support the design of valid assessments (Shute & Kee, 2012). Other researchers (Arnab et al., 2015; Hummel et al., 2017) present frameworks describing how to map the desired learning from a game (learning outcomes) to the game mechanics (gaming outcomes). Such models also emphasise the need to clearly specify the desired learning outcomes and translate these into linked game activities.

This paper describes an empirical study we carried out with the Youth@Work game (Boyle et al., 2016a; Hummel, Boyle, et al., 2015) as a potential solution for more experiential and active career learning. We developed this game to better motivate young people in exploring aspects of themselves and their potential occupations which is considered critical for enabling career decision making and development. Promoting a more active engagement is considered to be an important added value of game-based approaches besides traditional career counselling approaches (Amundson, 2003) and the available career information sites and systems (Sampson & Osborn, 2015). The game was developed as the main deliverable of the YOUTHYES project (Erasmus+ KA2, 2015—2017). We expect and hypothesise that playing this game will increase career awareness and adaptability in young people. From players in various countries we have collected both more qualitative and more quantitative data on their learning outcomes and satisfaction by conducting pre- and posttest questionnaires and by computer logging gaming data. This paper will focus on the more quantitative results that were obtained from a Randomized Controlled Trial that compared pre/post questionnaire scores on career awareness and adaptability (as main learning outcomes). The way we managed the challenge of balancing authenticity and playfulness in our game design is explained in the subsequent sections 2 and 3.

Section 2 (theoretical background) describes the most influential career counselling frameworks that were selected as an authentic and theoretical foundation for designing the main game structure (according to so called "zones"). Section 3 (method) contains a description of the Youth@Work game (play) and the assessment instrument for measuring learning outcomes. We explain how career counselling practice tasks have been mapped upon the learning scenario and its activities (into so called "mini-games"), and how feedback and scoring mechanisms have been unobtrusively integrated to ensure playful learning. We also describe our measuring instrument (that includes scales on career adaptability, awareness and learning). Sections 4 and 5 will present and discuss most important results from our controlled trial comparisons (before and after activity, between players and non-players, between countries), together with some recommendations for career counselling practice and future research.

分析：本文的前言部分比较长，第一段介绍了职业选择对于青少年今后职业发展的重要性以及目前青少年职业选择的困境，即目前的职业咨询方式对青少年没有吸引力。

第二、三段则介绍了所谓的"严肃游戏"（serious games）可以被用于职业咨询的实践中。作者引用文献表示，所谓的职业游戏正越来越多地被用作一种更具有激励性和更让人有身临其境感觉的方式，让学习者体验工作挑战，并评估他们在特定情境下的职业生活实践技能。在第三段中，作者明确提出他们要论证、开发并使用一款严肃职业游戏来支持年轻人的职业决策。

第四段主要介绍了这种职业游戏在设计时应注意的因素。比如，为了保证学习的真实性，游戏中的学习情境必须与学生应用所学内容的情境相似；而为了保证游戏化学习的趣味性，游戏玩法必须以一种不引人注目的方式整合个性化的反馈、支持和评分机制。

第五段中，作者介绍了该文所应用的一个名叫 Youth@Work 的职业游戏，并介绍了该游戏的开发目的，即更好地激励年轻人探索自己和探索他们的潜在职业的各个方面。接着，作者还介绍了本研究所采用的具体研究方法：预计并假设玩这个游戏将提高年轻人的职业意识和适应能力。通过对不同国家的玩家进行测试前和测试后的问卷调查，以及电脑记录游戏数据，收集了很多关于他们学习结果和满意度的定性和定量数据。从一项随机对照实验中获得了量化的结果，该实验比较了前问卷和后问卷中有关职业意识和职业适应能力的得分。在本段的最后，作者还提及在论文的第二、三章将探讨他们是如何在该游戏中平衡真实性和趣味性的。

前言的最后一段,作者简要介绍了后面各章的大致内容,这在一般的论文写作中并不常见(一般无须对后面各章进行说明)。作者表明,第二章是关于理论背景的描述(相当于文献回顾),介绍了最具影响力的职业咨询框架,这些框架被作者用作设计主要游戏结构的理论基础。而在第三章(即研究方法一章)中,作者对 Youth@Work 这一游戏做了说明,并介绍了用于衡量学习成果的评估工具。第四章和第五章则展示了研究结果并对结果进行了讨论(相当于论文中的研究结果和讨论这两章)。同时,作者在文章最后也对未来的职业咨询实践和研究方向给出了建议。

总体来看,本文的前言部分内容较为丰富,主要在于此处作者介绍了一些游戏化教学的相关内容(稍显过多,其实简单提一下即可,更深入的探讨可以放在文献回顾一章),并介绍了后面各章的内容(一般无须在前言部分介绍)。

第二部分:理论背景(Theoretical background)

Career learning and development is a long and complex process that has not been described in any coherent and integrated theoretical framework (e. g. Brown & Lent, 2013; Walsh, Savickas, & Hartung, 2013). Life-long guidance studies from Europe have focussed on career management skills and learning required (e. g. Law, 1996; Watts, 2001). We selected the Skills Development Scotland (SDS, 2012) framework to provide a broad overview of skills people need to manage their careers. From US studies that focussed on individual psychological differences and their measurement we know that when people choose an occupation that fits their interests, values and abilities in they feel more satisfaction with and are more successful in their careers (e. g. Savickas, 2005). We decided to use Holland's (1959, 1997) model of vocational interests because interests are considered especially important for career development (Savickas & Spokane, 1999). This section provides a description of both frameworks that theoretically underpin our game and define the main learning outcome variables: career adaptability, career awareness and perceptions of career learning and development.

2.1 *Skills development Scotland competence framework*

This first frameworkprovides a consistent definition of career management competences that young people need to be aware of in thinking about their careers, organised around four themes: Self: Competences that enable individuals to develop their sense of self within society; Strengths: Competences that enable individuals to acquire and build on their strengths and to pursue rewarding learning and work opportunities; Horizons: Competences that enable individuals to visualise, plan and achieve their aspirations throughout life; and Networks: Competences that enable individuals to develop relationships and networks of support. (see https://www.skillsdevelopmentscotland.co.uk/what-wedo/our-products/career-management-skills/) The SDS model seemed to provide an intuitive and useful framework for structuring the game into 4 zones, corresponding to these 4 different areas of competence, and also provided some indication of activities that might take place in these different zones. A final zone of the game, which was not part of the SDS competence framework, was required to provide an interesting conclusion to the game where the player finds out which of the careers he/she is most suited for.

2.2 *Holland's vocational interest model*

The second major career theory that was used in the game design was Holland's (1959, 1997) model of vocational interests. This theory is grounded in the study and measurement of individual differences, based on the premise that people who are able to choose an occupation that fits their interests will feel greater satisfaction and be more successful (Savickas & Spokane, 1999). Holland argued that vocational interests can be categorised in terms of six main RIASEC interest types: realistic, investigative, artistic, social, enterprising, and conventional.

Additionally, Prediger (1999) suggested that two bipolar dimensions (People-Things and Data-Ideas) underlie Holland's catergorization of vocational interests (see Figure 1). Interest inventories that measure the RIASEC interest types have been developed and used extensively in career guidance and counselling (Savickas & Spokane, 1999; Tracey & Sodano, 2013). The RIASEC categories have also been used to characterise actual careers in terms of the activities and skills required to perform different careers (see for example www.onetcenter.org). In the Youth@Work game, Holland's individual differences are nested in the proposed Self and Strengths Zones of the SDS Career management skills framework. Six representative professions were selected for each of the six RIASEC categories, leading to a collection of thirty-six possible careers that were implemented and elaborated in the matching algorithms of the game, using the gameplay information that was obtained in the first two game zones.

Our game design was also inspired by the research field of person-environment psychology (e.g. Walsh, Craik, & Price, 2000) where categorising and assessing individual difference characteristics are considered especially important for optimising the "fit" between the person and the requirement of a specific occupation. Working on that fit requires a psychosocial activity that has been conceptualised as "career adaptability" by Savickas (2005) and was defined as the attitudes, competences and behaviours that are needed to successfully fit yourself to suitable work. Playing the game is expected to raise the awareness of what choosing a career entails, to increase readiness, to provide learning and ultimately to increase career adaptability. Matching individuals' interests, abilitites and attainments to possible careers has been a feature of many career interest guides including Kudos (www. cascaid. co. uk/kudos), My World of Work (http://www. myworldofwork. co. uk/ and Futurewise (www. myfuturewise. org. uk).

分析：这一章是本文的文献回顾部分，分为两个小节。该章第一段概括介绍了为何本文采用2.1小节和2.2小节中的两个理论框架。大意为：本文将采用苏格兰技能发展框架(Skills Development Scotland，SDS，2012)来对人们管理职业所需要的技能做总体概述，并且文章也会采用Hollad(1959,1997)的职业兴趣模型，因为职业兴趣被认为对职业发展尤为重要。本章介绍的这两个框架构成了本文研究中使用的教学游戏的基石，并定义了主要的学习结果变量，即职业适应性、职业意识和对职业学习和发展的感知。

本章的2.1节介绍了苏格兰技能发展能力框架。作者认为这一框架给年轻人需要认识到的职业管理能力做了一个连贯的定义，框架围绕着四个主题：一是自我能力，即个人在社会发展中发展自我意识的能力；二是优势能力，即个人获得并建立起优势，并追求有价值的学习和工作机会的能力；三是视野能力，即个人在一生中进行想象、计划和实现抱负的能力；四是关系网能力，即个人建立和他人的关系和支持网的能力。作者认为苏格兰技能发展模型似乎可以为职业游戏提供一个直观和有用的框架，将该游戏按照该模型的4个能力主题分为4个区域，同时也可以指出哪些活动可以应用在这些不同的区域。本研究所使用的这个游戏还包含另外一个不在苏格兰技能发展框架内的区域，这一区域可以为游戏提供一个有趣的结论，玩家可以从中发现最适合自己的职业。作者不仅介绍了SDS框架，还对SDS框架和本研究的联系做了说明，否则审稿人可能会质疑：为何要在文中选择这一框架？

本章的2.2节分为3段，第1段介绍了本研究在设计教学游戏中用到的另一个职业理论，即Holland的职业兴趣模型。该模型扎根于对个人差异的研究和测量，其前提是"能够选择适合自己兴趣的职业会让人感到更有满足感，也会更成功。"Holland认为职业兴趣可以分为六种主要类型：实用型、研究型、艺术型、社会型、企业型和事务型(RIASEC)。本节的第2段介绍了Hollad理论和本研究的关系。作者认为在本研究使用的Youth@Work游戏中，Hollad理论中表述的个人差异被嵌套在前文提到的苏格兰职业管理技能框架的"自我能力"和"优势能力"两个区域里,并为每一个 Holland 兴趣类型选择了 6 种有代表性的职业,共计 36 种职业。这些职业在游戏中根据匹配算法进行了实现和描述。算法依据的就是在那两种能力区域中获得的信息。本章的第 3 段则介绍了该研究在设计教学游戏中牵涉到的其他一些理论,比如 Walsh 等人的"人—环境心理理论"等。作者最后认为,通过使用本研究的这一职业游戏,玩家可以提高职业选择中的内涵意识,提高玩家的职业准备能力,并最终提高他们的职业适应性。

第三部分:研究方法(Method)

We conducted a Randomized Controlled Trial in which participants were randomly assigned to one of two intervention conditions: half played the game, half executed a paper-and-pencil version (of the same activities in the game). Before and after the intervention questionnaires were provided to measure (perceived) change on career awareness and adaptabilities. The effects of the interventions were compared across condition and time, and analysed using descriptives, paired and independent t-tests and ANOVAs, that were calculated using SPSS version 22. Effects for potentially confounding variables like gender, age and country were controlled for. In the next subsections we now will describe: (1) the participants; (2) the procedure for administering questionnaires and interventions; (3) the interventions and (4) the scales of the questionnaire to measure outcomes and appreciation.

3.1 *Participants*

The Youth@work game had been initially targeted at a broad range of young people between the ages of 13 and 19 years who are starting to make decisions about which career they should follow. This includes school pupils (13-16 years old), college (16-19 years old) and even university students (18-24 years old) and those in work and NEETS (not in employment, education or training). However, during previous piloting of a Beta-release the game appeared most suitable for 13-16 years of age who are at the stage of making subject choices for their senior years in high school. The game can be played at home, but is probably best played with the support of a teacher or careers guidance advisor in a classroom context. Participants in this study were selected from that preferred context. Ninety-three high school students from Iceland (n=42, with 18 male and 24 female) and Romania (n=51, with 33 male and 18 female) were randomly assigned to playing the game (n=46) or doing a paper-and-pencil version of the same activity (n = 47) in classroom under supervision of their teacher /

counsellor. Their age range was 14-18 years (M=15.405, SD=1.019). We controlled for the effect of age, country and gender as possibly confounding covariables (see Results section).

3.2 *Procedure*

The teachers / counsellors of the high schools provided names and emails of participants to the researchers and reserved about two hours for executing the study in their scheduled classes about career counselling. Informed consent by parents was guaranteed beforehand, researchers anonymized the contact data into unique IDs and accounts, and randomly assigned these IDs to conditions. At the start of the class, the teacher / counsellor then explained the aim of the activity and divided these classes into two conditions, without informing them about the difference in treatment: one half played the activity (consisting of nine tasks) as a game (in their native language), while the other half executed the same activity and tasks (but without interactive game play and feedback, without the automatic calculation of matching scores in the last task) on paper (in their native language). The main differences between the experimental (game) and control (non-game) conditions were twofold: (a) participants in the control condition had to store and calculate their own scores on paper and did not automatically receive feedback, progress or matching scores based on these scores (therefore also could not do the last and ninth activity in the game); and (b) had to manually calculate their RIASEC vocational types (activity 7) and favourite jobs (activity 8) based on what they filled in as outcomes of activities 1-6. Game play outcomes were computer logged, the paper-and-pencil outcomes were collected on standardised worksheets (available in native languages) and stored in pdf format (these qualitative data were left out of scope for this more quantitative paper). It appeared that participants in both conditions on average took about an hour to complete the activity, so we did not have to control for time-on-task. Directly before and after the activity, participants had to fill in an online pre- and post-test questionnaire (both implemented in Google Form, in their native language), respectively, that had been matched to their unique ID/ account. Only Romanian participants considered the paper-and-pencil activity as a game and also filled in scale D of the post-test, and could be used as control group (n=25) for comparison with gamers that scored D items (n=44).

3.3 *Intervention*

The professional game we developed can be considered to be an adventure like game in which the player embarks on a (career) journey in search of the holy grail (which in this case is to find some valuable career advice). The game narrative starts with the player arriving by boat at the harbour of Job Fantasyland where the harbour master welcomes the weary traveller and provides instruction on how to travel across the island, with Crown Castle at the top of the island being the final destination (see first screengrab of Figure 2). In order to arrive there the player has to transverse the four zones (Self-Circus Cove, Strengths-Tiny Town, Horizons-Intercity and Networks-Intercity). In each zone the player is confronted with assistants who demand completion of certain tasks before the traveller is allowed to continue, with tasks provided in the form of mini-games. A total of 9 interactive mini-games are thus played in linear order, each with personalised feedback and scripted scoring and monitoring mechanisms in order to calculate progress and matching. The outcomes of the mini-games are stored in a personal journal (profile) and are also used to calculate scores on the RIASEC dimensions that guide the player in exploring specific career categories and then match with (a core set of 36) jobs. Finally, in Crown Castle, the traveller is handed over this personal journal by the King, together with job compatibility scores for the most relevant career options.

In the (five) mini-games in the first zones of the game (Circus Cove and Tiny Town), players are asked about themselves and their strengths, including which subjects they like most at school, what they like to do in their leisure-time (the Ferris wheel mini-game, see second screengrab of Figure 2), what they would value in a future career (the Mystic mini-game, see third screengrab of Figure 2), their personal qualities and their skills. The main aim of the Self and Strength zones was to find out about the players in an unobtrusive way. Players then progress to the (sixth) Networks mini-game, where the "Boss" invites them to take part in a workshop where they are asked to evaluate whether advice offered by 4 different people about 6 different career dilemmas is good or bad (see fourth and fifth screengrabs of Figure 2).

The aim of the Networks zone is to help players evaluate the quality of advice they are given about career decision making problems that they might encounter. In the Careers library in the Horizons zone, players take part in a (seventh) book sorting mini-game, where they help the librarian to sort out the muddled career books (see sixth screengrab of Figure 2). The 36 career books are arranged in 6 shelves (rows) according to RIASEC category. The aim of the library book sorting mini-game is to extend the player's knowledge that jobs differ with respect to certain characteristics. Players then have the opportunity to explore a number of careers in the eighth minigame, which are suggested on the basis of their responses in the first two zones of the game (see seventh screengrab of Figure 2), with the aim of further extending the player's knowledge about careers that might be of interest to them. Meanwhile all outcomes of playing the minigames are gradually filling up the pages of the personal journal (My Personal Profile, see eighth screengrab of Figure 2 and example in Table 1), in which scores on RIASEC categories and matches with jobs are calculated.

Crown Castle represents the end of the player's journey where they find out about their compatibility with the eight potentially most relevant jobs that were selected by playing the game. The "jobomatic" calculates matches based on the player's RIASEC score (derived from their leisure interests, subject preferences and personal qualities), as well as on their top 3 career values and skills ratings to the top 3 RIASEC categories, top 3 career values and 6 top skills for each job as described in O * Net. As players see compatibility scores for jobs the game is a kind of matching game, making recommendations about appropriate careers based on players' personalised responses. Although the game was set up as a linear sequence of tasks, we envisioned that having a narrative set up as adventure, meaningful personal choices feeding into personalisation of available information, interactivity with nonplaying characters that guide and advise players, and luck/chance in random advice are game dynamics that should be engaging and motivating for players.

The game was developed as open source in Unity, and is playable from Safari, Firefox and IE web browsers (although with the latter having slightly slower performance). It is available at http:// tinyoaks. ictthatworks. org/game/ JFL. html and needs an additional "unity web player" plugin to get installed. The web build runs in Chrome and is available at http://tinyoaks. ictthatworks. org/ game/ JFLWebGL/. Main advantages of using Unity are its potential for high-end GUI, and that it is easy to distribute as it is easily installed and cross platform. It is fully portable to tablets, androids and mobiles and also exportable to a website. A backdrop is its limited potential for more complex scripting of the narrative and feedback. The game dialogues were scripted initially in English, and later translated into (five) other languages (Icelandic, Romanian, Greek, Dutch and German).

3.4 Outcome measurement

Participants were asked to score (their perception of) three types of outcome measures: career adaptability, career awareness and readiness, and career learning and competences. Furthermore, they were asked to score how they had perceived game play itself.

3.4.1 Career adaptability

The Career Adapt-Abilities Inventory (CAAS 2.0) provides a well-researched and validated measurement instrument internationally (Savickas & Porfeli, 2012). The measure is based on a four dimensional conceptualisation of career adaptability: Curiosity, Concern, Control and Confidence (each containing six items; see Appendix 1, section A, items A1 till A24).

3.4.2 Career awareness and readiness

These two concepts were designed to capture career management skills development though the use of career websites by Howieson and Semple (2013), and were considered as important outcomes of playing the game. Items on Awareness and Readiness are presented in two separate sections each containing six items (see Appendix 1, sections E (items E63 till E68) and F (items F69 till F74)).

3.4.3 Career learning

Specific career learning was measured on two concepts, a motivational component measuring perceptions on career Learning containing seven questions (see appendix 1, section B, items B25 till B31) and 10 items where the youngsters were asked to evaluate their own career related learning Competences (see Appendix 1, section C, items C32 till C41).

3.4.4 Perceptions of the game

To evaluate the students' perceptions after playing the game (post-test only), we distinguished three concepts: Five items (D42 till D46) dealt with the possible Impact of the game on career learning and development; eleven items dealt with the Usability of playing the game (items D47 till D57); and the last four items (D58 till D61) dealt with game Features (such as graphics, narrative and characters (see Appendix 1, section D)).

分析：对于实证性论文来说，论文的研究方法这章一般需要交代实验对象的构成、实验步骤和实验中使用的工具等。本论文的这一部分被分为 4 个小节，分别是 3.1 实验对象、3.2 实验步骤、3.3 干预手段和 3.4 结果的测量。

本章第 1 段介绍了实验的大致设计和本章各小节的安排。可以看出本实验采取的是随机对照实验,实验对象被随机分配到两种干预条件中:一半的实验对象玩教学游戏,另一半实验对象进行的是该游戏对应的纸笔版的学习活动。在干预前后,对这些实验对象进行了问卷调查,以衡量(他们感知到的)在职业意识和职业适应能力方面的变化。本研究还对不同条件和时间内的干预手段的效果进行了比较,使用了描述性分析、配对和对立样本 T 检验、方差分析(ANOVA)等手段对实验数据进行了分析。同时,实验对于性别、年龄、国籍等潜在的混淆变量进行了控制。接下来,作者介绍了以下内容:3.1 节描述实验对象,3.2 节描述问卷发放和干预手段等的实验步骤,3.3 节描述干预手段,3.4 节描述采用哪些工具来对实验变量进行测量。

3.1 节介绍实验对象的信息。首先作者介绍了实验中使用到的那款 Youth@Work 的职业游戏可以应用的对象,包括各级别的学生(13~24 岁)、在职人员和啃老族,不过在试玩该游戏的 beta 版本后,作者发现这个游戏最适合 13~16 岁的高中生,因为他们正要为自己的高年级阶段选择科目。本研究的参与者正是从这样的群体中选择的。93 名高中生被选入本实验,分别来自冰岛(共 42 名学生,18 名男学生,24 名女学生)和罗马尼亚(共 51 名学生,33 名男学生,18 名女学生)。他们被随机分入玩游戏组(46 名学生)和游戏的纸笔版组(47 名学生),都在教室里接受老师或顾问的监督。参与者的年龄范围是 14~18 岁。实验对年龄、性别、国籍等可能的混淆协变量进行了控制(参见论文的研究结果一章)。

3.2 节介绍了实验的实施步骤。这些高中老师或顾问向本文的研究者提供了参与者的姓名和电子邮件,并在他们的职业咨询课上预留了 2 个小时进行此项实验。作者也提到,本研究在开始之初也取得了参与者家长的同意。研究者将学生的联系信息进行了匿名处理,形成独立的 ID 和账户,并随机将这些 ID 分配于不同的实验条件。在咨询课的开始,老师或顾问解释了本实验的目的,并将这些班级分成两种实验条件,但是并没有告知学生不同条件下的干预手段有何不同。一半的学生玩职业游戏(包括 9 个任务,母语版本),另一半的学生进行游戏的纸笔版活动(缺少游戏的互动和反馈,在最后一个任务中也不能对匹配分数进行自动计算,母语版本)。实验组(游戏化)和控制组(非游戏化)的主要区别包含两个方面:一方面是控制组的学生必须在纸上记录和计算自己的得分,他们无法自动获得各项分数的信息(所以他们无法进行游戏组里的最后一项和第 9 项活动);另一方面是控制组的学生必须基于在活动 1~6 中的得分手工计算自己的 RIASEC 职业类型(活动 7)和喜爱的工作(活动 8)。游戏组的结果是电脑保存的,而纸笔组的结果被记录在标准化的工作表中并以 PDF 格式保存。结果显示,两个组的参与者完成活动的平均时间都在一个小时左右,因此本研究不需要对任务时间进行控制。在活动前后,参与者都必须填写一份在线的问卷,这些问卷与他们独立的 ID/账户相匹配。只有罗马尼亚的参与者认为纸笔版的活动也属于游戏,所以他们也填写了后测中的 D 量表,因此他们可以被当作控制组(25 名学生)与填写了 D 量表的游戏玩家(44 名学生)进行对比。

3.3 节介绍了实验的干预手段,分为 5 段。第 1 段介绍了游戏的内容。该游戏是一款冒险游戏,玩家要展开一段寻找职业建议的旅程。游戏开始时,玩家乘船到达工作幻想世界的港口,在此处港口的主人向玩家们解释了如何穿越这个岛屿到达小岛顶端的皇冠城堡目的地——玩家必须经过 4 个区域(自我能力马戏团海湾、优势能力小镇、视野能力城际站和关系网能力城际站)才可以到达。在每个区域,玩家都要完成一些任务后才能继续进行游戏,这些任务都是以迷你游戏的方式呈现的。玩家总共要按照线性顺序玩 9 个迷你游戏,每个游戏都会有个性化的反馈、脚本化的评分和控制机制,以便计算游戏进度和匹配。这些迷你游戏的结果被存储在个人日志中,并被用于计算其 RIASEC 维度的分数,该维度指导玩家探索特定的职业类别,然后与 36 个核心职业进行匹配。最后,在皇冠城堡,国王将这本个人日志连同与该玩家最相关的职业选择的匹配分数一起交给这名玩家。

3.3 小节的第 2、3、4 段则对游戏里的各环节做了更为详尽的介绍。第 2 段介绍了玩家在自我能力马戏团海湾、优势能力小镇和关系网能力城际站遇到的任务。在前两个区域,玩家将被问及他们的个人信息和优势能力,以及他们在学校擅长的科目、休闲时的活动和对未来职业价值的考量。随后,玩家就进入关系网能力的迷你游戏环节。此处,游戏中的"老板"邀请玩家参加一个工作坊,玩家需要评估 4 个人提供的有关 6 个职业困境的建议。在第 3 段,文章首先介绍了关系网区域游戏的目的是帮助玩家评估自己得到的职业建议的质量。在视野能力区域的职业图书馆内,玩家们参加一个图书分类小游戏,他们要帮助图书管理员整理混乱的职业书籍——根据 RIASEC 分类标准将 36 本职业书籍放在书架的 6 个隔板上。图书分类任务主要是扩展玩家对职业特征的了解。接着,在第 8 个小游戏中,玩家们得以探索几种职业,这些职业都是依据玩家们在前两个游戏区域中的回答而推荐的,这一游戏的目的仍然是扩展玩家们对于职业的了解。与此同时,这些小游戏的结果都被记录在个人日志里,而个人日志还会对每个玩家的 RIASEC 分类和与工作的匹配度进行评分。在第 4 段,文章介绍了游戏的目的地——皇冠城堡。在皇冠城堡,玩家们可以看到自己与游戏中选择的 8 个最相关工作的匹配度。游戏会根据玩家的 RIASEC 得分(基于玩家的业余兴趣、科目偏好和个人素质)、依据 RIASEC 分类的前 3 类评出的玩家的前 3 项职业价值和技能得分,以及依据 O*Net(美国职业信息网络)里每一个工作评出的前 3 项职业价值和前 6 项技术来计算玩家的职业匹配。作者指出,这个游戏就是配对游戏,依据玩家的个性化回应来推荐适合他们的职业。虽然该游戏是线性化的任务,但是冒险因素、互动、运气/机会等随机因素都会让该游戏具有吸引力和激励性。

本节最后一段介绍了该游戏的运行环境,作者指出该游戏可以被移植到平板电脑、安卓系统和手机上,潜力巨大。

3.4节介绍了本研究对于实验结果的测量,又分为4个小节。第1段为概括段落,文章介绍参与者被要求对3种衡量标准进行打分,即职业适应能力、职业意识和准备程度、职业学习和能力。此外,参与者还需要对游戏本身评分。

3.4.1小节介绍对职业适应能力的评分。本研究采用了职业适应力量表(CSSA 2.0)作为工具。该量表基于4个维度:好奇心、关注度、控制和信心,每个维度包含6个项目(见该文的附录1,A部分,A1～A24项目)。3.4.2小节介绍了对职业意识和准备程度的评分。这两个量表每个也包含6个项目(分别见该文附录1的E部分,E63～E68项目,和附录1的F部分,F69～F74项目)。3.4.3小节介绍了对职业学习的评分。量表分为两个部分,分别是附录1的B部分,包含7个项目(针对职业学习的动机),和附录1的C部分,包含10个项目(要求参与者为自己的职业学习能力进行评分)。3.4.4小节介绍了对游戏本身的评分。研究区分了3个概念,分别是该游戏对职业学习和发展的影响(D42～D46项目)、该游戏的可用性(D47～D57)和该游戏的特色(D58～D61,包括游戏图形、叙事和角色)。

第四部分:研究结果(Results)

This section presents our main findings on the effects of the intervention over time and differences between conditions, but first explains how we checked for potentially spurious effects of baseline differences and co-variates.

4.1 *Control for baseline differences and co-variates*

We confirmed that pre-test scores for both conditions were not already different as baseline. Before running our comparative analyses we ensured that all questionnaire items within the same (sub) scale had the same (positive or negative) direction in order to meaningfully calculate averages. Six items of the questionnaire (B26, B30, D47, D51, D54, D58, see Appendix 1) had to be transposed, with higher averages on scores A-D and lower averages on scores E-F to be interpreted as more positive outcomes. No differences were found for co-variates age, gender and country on the scores A-F of the pre-test. Significant differences on the independent samples t-test were found for gender on the C scores of the post-test ($M_{male}=4.068$, $M_{female}=4.167$, with $p<0.05$), and for country on both the E score ($M_{Iceland}=1.833$, $M_{Romania}=3.281$, with $p<0.01$) and the F score ($M_{Iceland}=1.850$, $M_{Romania}=3.408$, with $p<0.01$) of the post-test. Please note that high scores on A-D scales are "positive" and high scores on E-F scales are "negative".

4.2 *Effects of the intervention over time*

A paired samples t-test comparing the pre and post test scores on scales A,

B、C、E and F (see Table 2) shows significant (short-term) growth over all participants on the average scores for A with $t(89) = -2.816$ and $p<0.01$, and for C with $t(89) = -1.992$ and $p<0.05$, but shows decreases (however not significant) on B and E. Scores tend to increase on scales A、C and F (the last not being significant), and tend to decrease on scales B and E (both not significant) over time.

4.3 *Effects of experimental condition*

When looking for an effect of condition (gamers versus non-gamers) on the average post-test scores on the main scales A-F (see Table 2), no significant differences could be found for B、C、E and F. At the level of the scales, only an effect of condition was found for A (Career Adaptability) with $F(1,88) = 6.662$, $p<0.05$, h2 $p=0.071$. However, when looking for the effect of condition on the level of subscales, we did find significant and positive developments on three out of the four career adaptability dimensions (subscales A): for "concern" with $F(1,88) = 10.321$, $p<0.01$, h2 $p=0.105$), for "control" with $F(1,88) = 8.180$, $p<0.01$, h2 $p=0.085$, and for "confidence" with $F(1,88) = 2.188$, $p<0.05$, h2 $p = 0.034$. An effect of condition was also found on the D subscale "perceptions of game features" with $F(1,67) = 2.946$, $p<0.01$, h2 $p=0.081$. These partial-eta-squared values, according to Cohen's guidelines for interpretation (1988), can be considered as medium to large effect sizes.

4.4 *Qualitative views on the game*

Participants could verbally express their own views on playing the game at the end of the questionnaire. We present some quotes that might illustrate the benefits of playing the game. Comments provided were generally positive and mostly related to the usability of the game (like: "I liked how easy it was to use") and players' views about the game features (like "The characters were nice and they made the instructions easy to follow"; "The images were nice and colourful"). Positive views were also expressed about the benefits and impact of the game (like: "Great way to learn about careers", "Especially liked being taken on a journey"; "It was a very useful and motivating way to learn about myself"; "I very much liked to find out about all the jobs I was compatible fo in this way"; "I think it's a good way to find out about your skills / more about yourself in a fun way"; "I like that it encourages you to think about values, preferences almost indirectly").

分析：本文的研究结果一章分成 4 个小节。第 1 段为总体介绍，指出本章将会介绍干预手段随时间和条件的变化而产生的影响,但是文章首先将会介绍如何检验基线差异和协变量潜在的虚假效应。

4.1节说的是对基线差异和协变量的控制。文中提到,两种条件下的前测分数作为基线没有差异,而且在进行比较分析前本实验的研究人员会确保相同的量表(或子量表)的项目具有相同的正负向。问卷中有6个项目(该文附录1中的B26、B30、D47、D51、D54、D58)必须要转置,因为A~D量表得分高和E~F量表得分低都意味着更为正面的结果。年龄、性别和国籍这些协变量在前测的A~F量表上的得分没有发现差异。然而,国籍这一协变量在后测的E量表和F量表上的得分却通过独立样本T检验发现具有显著差异。

4.2节介绍了对前、后测的A、B、C、E、F量表进行配对样本T检验的情况,结果发现所有的参与者在A、C两个量表的得分都是显著增加的,而在B、E两个量表的得分却降低了(虽然不显著)。总之,不同的干预手段随着时间变化会造成A、C、F量表的得分倾向于增加(F量表得分不显著),而B、E两个量表的得分倾向于降低(均不显著)。

4.3节介绍了两种实验条件(游戏模式和非游戏模式)的影响。研究发现后测中的B、C、E、F量表的得分均没有差异,只有子量表的得分有显著差异。然而,在A量表的4个子量表中有3个(关注、控制、信心)都发现了显著差异。D量表的"对于游戏特色的看法"子量表得分也有显著差异。而且,根据Cohen(1988)的说法,这些差异都具有中到大的效应量。

本章的最后一节介绍了参与者在问卷最后表达的对游戏的看法。文章指出,玩家对该游戏的评论基本都是正面的,并且多数评价都与游戏的可用性和功能相关。还有的玩家对于应用该游戏的好处和影响也表达了积极的看法。

从第4章的小节安排来看,其内容安排基本上是按照第3章的3.4节来进行的。这就提醒我们,文章需要前后呼应。一般来说,研究结果的呈现需要和前面提出的研究问题(或者研究假设)进行对应。不过各论文的章节安排未必完全一样,如本文就没有单独的"研究问题"(Research questions)一章,但是其研究结果还是与前文提出的话题进行了对应。

第五部分:结论与讨论(Conclusion and Discussion)

Careful consideration of two career theories was helpful to theoretically ground and validate learning outcomes of the Youth@Work game, with the SDS model of career competences providing guidance about the organisation of the game and the different zones and Holland's model of vocational interests identifying activities for the different zones. Inclusion of dynamic and engaging game mechanics that include an adventure like narrative, personalised choice, interaction, progression and scoring, along with the "matching" idea that required progression on finding out about yourself and careers and then looking at the match between these, were considered to foster career awareness and capability.

As we found the use of game-based learning in career counselling practice to have been scarce, the aim of this study was to research the added value of providing career decision making activity in such a more interactive and experiential way (i.e. gamers versus non-gamers). We stress that we consider gaming as complementary to current career counselling practice, and did not want to compare more classic and more innovative practices (e.g. gaming versus interviews).

Main results of the comparisons over time (pre- and post-test scores) and between condition (gamers versus non-gamers) show that participants mostly report positive change after doing the career activity. Significant positive effects over time were found for career adaptability (scale A) and perception on career learning competences (scale C). Not finding any more substantial change over time is not that surprising considering the short time lapse (about an hour) between pre- and post-testing. On the level of main scales, a significant (additional) effect for gaming was found for career adaptability (scale A). Furthermore, we were able to identify significant differences between conditions (the added value of carrying out the activities in a more dynamic and engaging way) on the A subscale dimensions "concern", "control" and "confidence" (but not on "curiosity"). This means that players reported significantly better sense of control of and concern and confidence about careers after game play when compared to non-gamers. Finally and not surprisingly, game features (of the activity) were scored better by gamers than by non-gamers.

Besides the small time-frame of the study, limitations in further growth might be caused by other reasons. Savickas and Porfeli (2012) reported big differences in the discriminative power of the CAAS instrument across countries (generally being more discriminative for Asian countries and less so for European countries). Overall, pre-test scores on the A-C scales were relatively high (and socially desirable) so there might be a "ceiling effect" on further growth. Furthermore, scales B, C and D were not validated (nor grounded in theory) so might not measure what we intended.

Finally, we were left with some intriguing questions like: Why are Icelandic students more positive about growth on career awareness and readiness (scales E and F) after the activity? and Why do girls have more positive perceptions about career learning competences (scale C) after the activity? Regarding the first issue, it is possible that Icelandic students consider themselves more aware of their career opportunities and more ready for decision making, due to the character of their educational system (demanding frequent choices) or their labour market (with a high youth employment), in comparison with their Romanian counterparts. Or they might be a bit more overconfident or "yea-saying." Regarding the last issue about gender differences on the career learning (scale C), our educated guess is that girls overall are more conscientious students than boys and therefore more willing to engage in the presented activities, and more apt to learn in the process.

Further studies should extend these findings by including interventions and measurements in longer time-frames to see if these outcomes change more over time. Although in this study we did encounter only minor differences between two countries, including more countries in the population would be informative (e.g. Howieson & Semple, 2013). Where the main source of data collection in this study was questionnaires, future game design should enable more objective outcome data to be collected by in-game performance measures. Most important scales used in the questionnaire are based on validation in prior research, but not all. Triangulation of data collection methods, like combining questionnaire results with focussed interviews, observations of playing behaviour, computer logging of progress and performance, and others might shed more light on some of the findings we could not explain. Replicating this study in other contexts of use (beyond the classroom, in more informal or non-formal contexts of career construction) would also be interesting and advisable. The finding from this study that game-based learning is appreciated as (at least) equal to more classical instruction with paper-and-pencil testing, is promising in its own right when looking for the benefits of more time- and place-independent career advice support. Additional growth for gamers on their sense of control, concern and confidence about their careers can be considered as a promising result when considering game-based learning for the career counselling practice.

分析:本文将结论和讨论放在一章,这种安排并不太常见。一般来说,这两个部分是各成一章的。此外,讨论部分是论文最重要也是最难写的一章,所以通常都是单独成章,以便对实验结果进行深层次的探讨。在本章的前六段,作者对于本研究的发现做了总结并讨论,最后一段则对未来的研究提出建议。

第一段重申苏格兰职业能力模型和 Holland 职业兴趣模型给本研究奠定了坚实的基础。

第二段介绍为何本研究要采用游戏化教学的方式,原因在于目前基于游戏的学习在职业咨询实践中应用得很少,而本研究就是要探究这一更具互动性和体验性的教学方式给职业决策活动带来的附加价值。作者还申明,游戏化教学只是对当前职业咨询实践的补充,本研究并不想在经典实践(面试)和创新实践(游戏)之间进行比较。

第三段则对本次实验的主要结果做了讨论。首先,作者再次阐述了主要发现,主要是参与者在进行了这些游戏活动后大多数都有了积极的变化,干预手段对职业适应性(A 量表)、对职业学习能力的感知(C 量表)都有显著的积极影响。其他方面没有发现根本变化可能是由于本研究的执行时间很短(前后测之间只隔 1 个小时)。而且,A 量表的 4 个维度中有 3 个(关注、控制和信心)都被发现产生了显著差异。这意味着与非游戏玩家相比,游戏玩家在游戏结束后对职业的掌控感、关注感和自信心明显增强。与此同时,游戏玩家比非游戏玩家对游戏功能的评分也更高。

第四段介绍了其他一些可能限制了干预手段效果的因素。如本研究采用的 CAAS(The Career Adapt-Abilities Inventory,职业适应能力量表)工具就会在各国显示出不同的歧视程度(一般来说,亚洲国家比欧洲国家的歧视程度更高)。总体来看,A~C 量表的前测分数相对较高,所以可能会对干预手段的进一步增长产生"天花板效应"。此外,B、C、D 量表并没有经过验证,所以它们可能无法测量研究的真正目标。

在第五段,文章澄清了一些可能的疑问,如"为什么冰岛学生在参加了活动后对职业意识和准备程度的增长(E 和 F 量表)有更正面的看法?""为什么女生在活动后对职业学习能力(C 量表)有更正面的认知?"作者对这两个疑问,提供了可能的解释。

作者在本章最后一段对未来的此类研究提出了建议,其实这些建议也可以看作是当前研究的不足。例如,作者认为未来的研究可以采用更长的时间,以便观察干预手段是否会随着时间的变化产生更大的变化。作者还建议,未来的研究可以包含更多不同国家的实验对象和未来的研究应设计更多的数据来源,而不像本研究主要依靠问卷调查。这一段的最后两句又对本文的研究结果做了总结。作者表明,本研究发现游戏化的学习至少与传统的纸笔式教学同等重要,更可以被用来寻求那些与时间和地点无关的职业建议。而且，将这种游戏化的学习方式应用于职业咨询实践更有可能进一步增强这些游戏玩家对职业的控制能力、关注度和信心。

2.12 SSCI论文常用表达方式

我们在阅读SSCI期刊刊登的论文时会发现，很多文章在进行某些表达时有相同之处，而某些词汇在使用上又需要多加注意。本节介绍一些常用的表达形式。要注意的是，下面提到的表达形式只是常用的，并不表示写作时必须使用这些表达方式。

1) 如何表达"本研究/本文"

常用词汇：**this/the present/the current** study/research/paper/article

例文："**The present article** makes a distinctive contribution……"（大意：本文做出了明显的贡献……）(Dowling & Whiteman, 2020)

2) 如何表达"促进了/提高了/提升了"

常用词汇：**improve/facilitate/enhance/promote**

例文："Please suggest actions that might **enhance** the relationship between education researchers and research ethics committees."（大意：请推荐一些可能增进教育研究者和研究伦理委员会之间关系的举措。）(Brown, Spiro, & Quinton, 2020)

3) 如何表达"提出/表明/描述/暗示"

常用词汇：**suggest/indicate/show/denote/depict/point out/imply/indicate**

例文1："The data in Table 2 **indicates** that the participants in this study conduct research with a number of different groups and arenas associated with education."（大意：表2中的数据表明，本研究的参与者对好几个与教育相关的不同群体和领域进行了研究。）(Brown, Spiro, & Quinton, 2020)

例文2："Frequently, those relationships among nodes can be **depicted** in a social network diagram."（大意：通常，节点之间的关系可以用社交网络图来描述。）(Lee & Bonk, 2016)

4) 如何表达"说明/解释"

常用词汇：**illustrate/explain/clarify**

例文："SNA has commonly been used as a major data analysis method in educational research to **illustrate** different variables such as relationship, emotion, help, and other social phenomena."（大意：SNA（社交网络分析）在教育

研究中通常被用作主要的数据分析方法来解释不同的变量,如关系、情感、帮助等社会现象。)(Lee & Bonk,2016)

5) 如何表达"证实/证实/呼应"

常用词汇:confirm/testify/prove/echo/support/be consistent with/concur with

例文1:"Instead of solely relying on self-reported data, as seen in similar research, this study also **confirmed** that online interactions are positively correlated with closeness among peers based on their actual activities for the 16 weeks of the course."(大意:与在类似研究中看到的完全依赖自我报告的数据不同,这项研究也证实了在为期16周的课程中,通过实际活动,学习同伴的在线互动与他们之间的亲密度呈正相关。)(Lee & Bonk,2016)

例文2:"This view was **echoed** by another study that employed a microworld-based role-playing game to teach mathematics."(大意:这一观点得到了另一项研究的回应,该研究采用了一个基于微观世界的角色扮演游戏来教授数学。)(Ge,2019)

例文3:"As expected, the responses from the students **were consistent with** the previous studies reporting that blogging can overcome a sense of isolation (Hall & Davidson, 2007) and create a stronger sense of community (Dickey, 2004; Nardi et al., 2004)."(大意:正如预期的那样,学生的反应与前人的研究一致,这些研究指出博客可以克服孤立感(Hall & Davidson,2007),并创造更强的社区意识。(Dickey,2004;Nardi 等,2004))(Lee & Bonk,2016)

例文4:"This **concurs with** Faucher and Caves (2009) who noted that misconduct in exams often occurs when 'opportunities are provided and surveillance is minimized'."(大意:这与Faucher和Caves(2009)的观点一致,他们指出,在"作弊的机会被提供,而监督被最小化"时,考试中的不当行为就会发生)(Hylton,Levy,&Dringus,2016)

6) 如何表达"目的是……"

常用词汇:aims to/be to…

例文:"Thus, this study **aims to** explore researcher perceptions of research ethics committees as friend or foe in educational research, addressing a gap in current research."(大意:因此,本研究旨在探讨研究者对研究伦理委员会在教育研究中是敌是友的看法,以弥补当前研究的空白。)(Brown,Spiro,& Quinton,2020)

7) 如何表达"推翻了/否定了/驳斥了"

常用词汇:repudiate/refute/reject/contradict

例文1:"Rather, they typically seek to prove the superiority of their own arguments and **refute** their opponents' arguments."(大意:相反,他们通常试图证明自己论点的优越性,并反驳对手的论点。)(Lin, Fan, & Xie, 2020)

例文2:"These results **contradict** previous findings indicating a positive correlation between pornography use and body dissatisfaction in sexual minority men, and further research is needed to explore these discrepancies."(大意:这些结果与先前的研究结果相矛盾,即在性少数群体的男性中,色情作品的使用与身体不满意之间存在正相关关系。需要进一步的研究来探究这些差异。)(Gleason & Sprankel, 2019)

8) 如何表达"如下"

常用表达:**as follows**

例文:"Therefore, how metacognition relates to the three levels of Chinese learning interest in MOOCs was hypothesized **as follows**."(大意:因此,元认知和利用慕课进行汉语学习的学习兴趣的三个层次之间的关系假设如下。)(Tsai, Lin, Hong, & Tai, 2019)

9) 如何表达"调查/探讨/了解……"

常用表达:**discuss/investigate/probe into**…

例文:"First, the present study is one of the few studies to **probe into** the association between workplace ostracism and employee creativity."(大意:首先,本研究是探讨职场排斥与员工创造力之间关系的少数研究之一。)(Tu, Cheng, & Liu, 2019)

10) 如何表达"导致/产生"

常用表达:**lead to/elicit/trigger**

例文1:"Different functions of platforms may **lead to** different demonstrations of learning content and may **trigger** different types of interactivity."(大意:不同的平台功能可能会导致学习内容的演示不同,并可能会引发不同类型的交互。)(Tsai, Lin, Hong, & Tai, 2019)

例文2:"This result suggests that the forfeit-or-prize reward pattern was the best at **eliciting** good knowledge retention results among the three patterns."(大意:这一结果表明,在三种奖励模式中,奖惩结合的模式在产生良好的知识记忆效果方面效果最好。)(Ge, 2018)

11) 如何表达"达成一致"(本节第5条的词语也可以酌情使用)

常用表达:**consensus on**…

例文:"However, there is no **consensus on** the designs of educational games, because educational settings and educational purposes are varied and frequently changing."(大意:然而,对于教育游戏的设计并没有一致的意见,因为教育的情境和教育的目的是多种多样的并且经常变化的。)(Ge, 2019)

12) 如何表达"提出/宣称"

常用表达:**propose/claim/declare/assert**

例文1:"It is **claimed** that ethical regulation has been implemented to protect universities and other organisations from litigation…"(大意:据称,道德规范的实施是为了保护大学和其他组织免受诉讼……)(Brown, Spiro, & Quinton, 2020)

例文2:"Thus, it is not surprising that many educators **assert** that programming is important for K-12 students in this era."(大意:因此,许多教育工作者断言,在这个时代编程对 K-12 学生很重要,这并不奇怪。)(Lye & Koh, 2014)

13) 如何表达"开展了/执行了/实施了/采用了"

常用表达:**adopt/apply/administer/carry out**

例文1:"Educators in science education reported there are basically two kinds of argumentative goals can be **adopted** in school science teaching: persuasion, and consensus."(大意:科学教育的教育者认为,学校科学教学中可以采用的争论目标主要有两种:说服对方和达成共识)(Lin, Fan, & Xie, 2020)

例文2:"**Administer** a pre-test to check students' readiness for the in-class Activities."(大意:对学生进行预考,检查他们是否为课内活动做好了准备。)(Wang, 2017)

2.13 SSCI 论文参考文献的获取与使用

在学术论文的写作中,参考文献的使用是必不可少的。但是有一个棘手的问题:由于期刊对于参考文献的引用格式可能存在差异,使得我们在投稿时可能需要根据这些要求不断地对文献格式进行调整,这是一个相当烦琐的过程。此外,如何获取需要的参考文献呢?本小节就来谈谈参考文献的获取与使用。

首先,我们来看如何获取和论文主题相关的参考文献。一种方法是直接在谷歌学术网站上根据论文的关键词搜索。例如,论文主题是 game-based learning,我们只需要在谷歌学术页面中输入这一关键词即可(如图 2-4 所示)。在图 2-4 中,我们看到页面左侧可以对文献的年代进行筛选,而页面右侧的[PDF]标志则表示该文献可以获取原文。此外,可以点击谷歌学术页面右上角的三条横线处进行高级搜索。

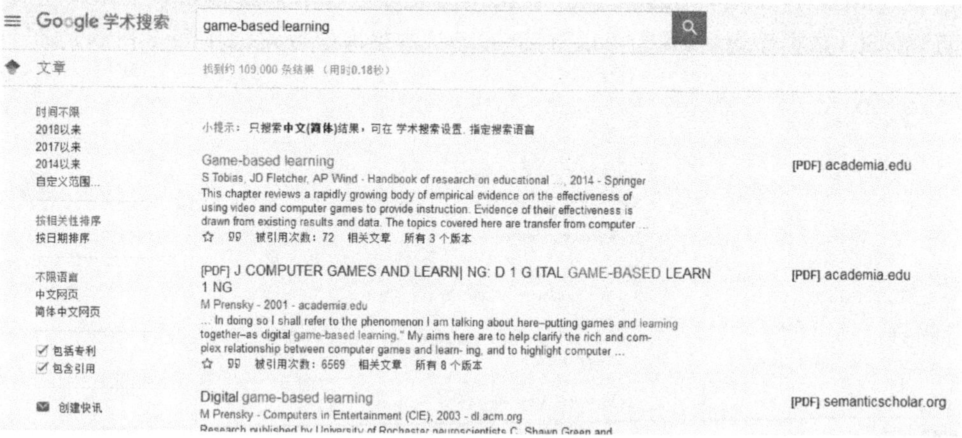

图 2-4　在谷歌学术进行文献搜索

接下来，我们看看如何利用百度学术进行文献搜索。同样，我们也只需要将关键词输入即可（如图 2-5 所示）。我们可以看到，在百度学术的页码左侧提供了更多的筛选项目。

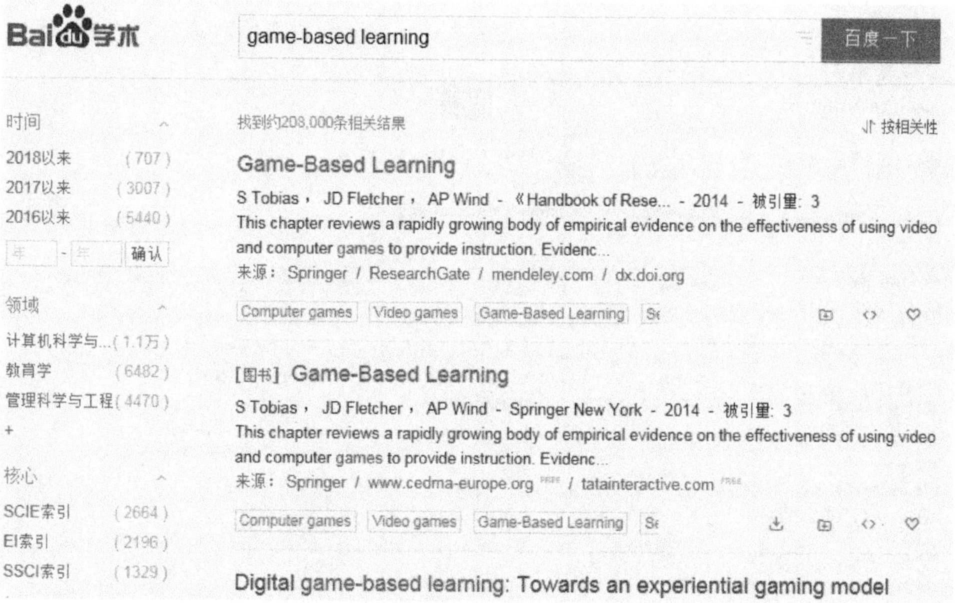

图 2-5　在百度学术中进行文献搜索

除了这两种比较常见的聚合类文献搜索引擎之外，我们还可以在某些学术数据库中进行搜索，如 https://www.sciencedirect.com/search/advanced（如图 2-6

所示)、https://link.springer.com/search（如图2-7所示），或者如果工作单位有订购SSCI数据库的话，我们可以直接在SSCI数据库中搜索（如图2-8所示）。

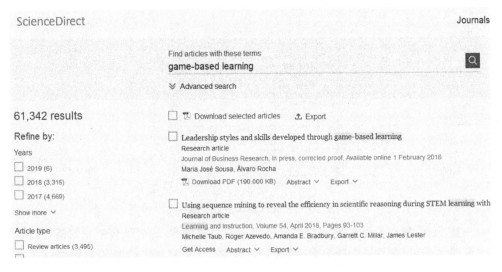

图2-6　在Sicencedirect中搜索文献

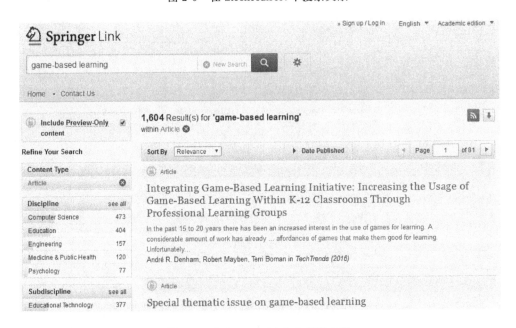

图2-7　在SpringerLink中搜索文献

第 2 章　SSCI 论文的结构与写作

图 2-8　在 SSCI 数据库中检索文献

检索文献后，我们无法将所有的文献完整下载，因为很多文献都是收费的，不过这些文献的摘要都是免费可见的，由于摘要是对文章的高度概括，所以通过阅读摘要，我们可以知道该文献适不适合引用。举两个例子，第一例是谷歌学术中搜索到的文献，点开一篇文章查看摘要，一般来说，点击后页面会直接跳转到该文章在线出版的网址（如图 2-9 所示）。点击谷歌学术中的这篇文章后直接跳转到该文章发表期刊的网页，该网页上有这篇期刊的详细信息，包括摘要、作者、文章结构等。页面上方的"Export"按钮允许我们导出该文章的引用格式，点击后看到如图 2-10 所示的界面。我们可以依据自己使用的文献引用软件（如 Mendely、endnote）等进行设置，导出该文章的引用信息，然后直接在文献引用软件中使用。

图 2-9　跳转的文章网页

图 2-10　文献引用链接

　　需要注意的是,有的数据库(尤其是百度学术)中文献的信息并不准确,主要是文献的发表时间有偏差,这是因为很多文章在被期刊接收后随即产生 Online First 版本(在线优先版本),而该文章正式出版的时间和 Online First 版本不同,我们在引用时最好使用该文章的正式出版时间。针对这一可能的现象,解决办法是:搜索到该文章后一定要去刊发该文的杂志官网页面进行确认。

第 3 章 从投稿到发表

3.1 稿件状态

当我们在目标期刊的投稿系统里点击"Submit"按钮之后,稿件就进入了该期刊的投稿数据库了。不同的投稿系统,稿件的状态是不同的,如 Elsevier 投稿系统,投稿后有的期刊会立刻分配稿号,而有的期刊则是在文章通过了技术审查(Technical Check)之后才会分配稿号,然后又会出现 With Editor(分配编辑)、Under Review(评审)、Revise With Extensive Work(大修)等状态。这里没有必要对每一个状态作出详细解释,因为不仅不同的投稿系统会稍有区别,即便是同一个投稿系统里不同的期刊也可能会有区别。总之,作为投稿者,只要系统中没有出现"Reject"(拒稿),我们能做的就是等待。等待的结果,最坏的就是"Reject"(拒稿),除此之外,编辑给出的决定基本都是让修改。即使等来的结果是"Reject & Resubmit"(拒稿重投),这也不表示论文被拒了,而是可以修改后再次投向该期刊的。如果等来的结果是"Reject",那么只能考虑投别的期刊了。图 3-1 和图 3-2 分别显示了 Elsevier 系统和 Evise 系统给出的"Major Revision"决定的界面(图中的大修文章已经返回了)。图 3-1 中的"R1"指的是该文章是第 1 次修改。

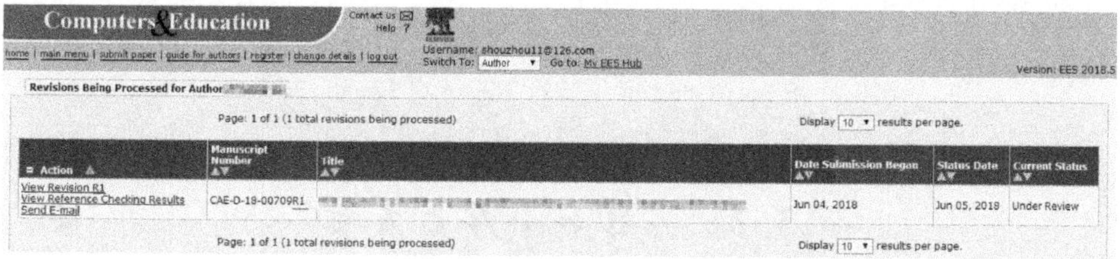

图 3-1 Elsevier 投稿系统的大修界面

而图 3-2 则显示了 Evise 投稿系统的大修界面,其中的"R1"指的是第 1 次大修,该系统还显示了大修返回的最迟期限(Revision response due date)。

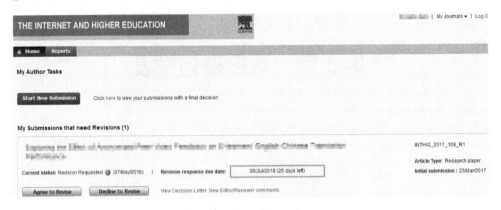

图 3-2　Evise 投稿系统的大修界面

图 3-3(ScholarOne 投稿系统的"reject & resubmit"界面)则给出了 ScholarOne 投稿系统中"Reject & Submit"(拒稿重投)后返回修改稿的界面。可以看出,该作者已经返回了修改稿,而且修改稿被重新分配了稿号(初稿稿号是 RIIE-2018-0079,而重投稿稿号是 RIIE-2018-0167)。

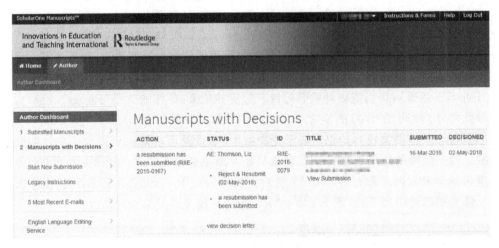

图 3-3　ScholarOne 投稿系统的"Reject & Resubmit"界面

3.2　大修和小修的应对

经过几个月,甚至是一年左右的等待后,最兴奋的莫过于收到编辑邀请作者对文章进行修改的信件了。文章被直接接受的情况很少发生,大多数作者都要对文章进行一轮或多轮的修改。修改时,作者需要对编辑和审稿人的意见作出一对一的回复(Point-to-point Response),写一份审稿意见应答信(Response to Reviewers' Comments),这些回复需要在提交修改稿时一并提交到系统里。本小节主要谈谈如何回复审稿人的意见。

1)审稿人提出的语法、拼写等错误

针对这种审稿意见,作者的回复一般都是全盘接受,并在应答信里附上修改后的一两个例子。如果作者实在对自己的语言功底没有把握,也可以付费使用专业的论文润色公司提供的服务。

2)审稿人提出的论文语句逻辑性方面的问题

此类意见很让人头疼,但是必须按照意见对语句进行逐一检查,看看句子之间、段落之间的语意连接有没有问题,若有问题则要一一进行改正。这种问题,一般来说只能是作者自己来改,或者求助英语比较好的朋友与其一起修改。

3)参考文献的问题

审稿人可能会让作者增加某些文献的引用,或者让作者对某些文献进行更详尽的阐述。

4)数据统计方法的问题

人文社科类实证研究经常用到数据统计。当审稿人提出诸如"是用独立样本T检验还是用配对样本T检验""得到的数据结果如何解读"等问题时,作者应先检查自己的统计方法是否有问题,如果有问题要按照审稿意见进行修改;如果统计方法没有问题,在回复审稿人时,一定要进行解释,最好能附上几篇使用了相似统计方法的已发表论文作为证明。例如,笔者的一篇论文是比较一种新的教学方法和传统的教学方法在教学效果上的差异,试验分成了两个组(Group A 和 Group B),对后测进行了独立样本T检验,可是审稿人认为应该用配对样本T检验。笔者回复如下:

As for the statistical tests, I am afraid that a paired-sample T-test is not appropriate for my study. Let me explain the difference between a paired-sample T-test and an independent-sample T-test: *An Independent T-Test* is used to examine if there is a difference in the means of *two DIFFERENT groups* (i.e. Independent variable: Group 1: Police Officers/ Group 2: Soldiers. Dependent Variable: Levels of aggression). You are testing if there is a difference between the level of violence carried out as a result of the groups the participants identify with. While *a Paired Samples T-Test* is to test if there is a difference in the levels of aggression between the members of *only ONE group*. The SAME participants are measured at different time intervals and compared (1. e. Time 1/

Time 2/ Time 3).

You may find another example at https://help. xlstat. com/customer/en/portal/articles/2062455-what-is-the-difference-between-paired-and-independent-samples-tests-? b_id=9283.

You can find the explanation to paired samples T-test at https://libguides. library. kent. edu/SPSS/PairedSamplestTest.

As my study is to compare the means of two different groups (Group A and Group B), an independent-sample T-test is more appropriate.

在上面的回复信中，笔者引用前人论文中的实验设计来支持自己的实验设计，并给出了相关链接供审稿人查看。此外，为了确保二审时编辑不会被审稿人的这种错误意见误导，作者在提交修改稿时，可以在给编辑的投稿信里将审稿人的错误一一指出。例如，笔者在返回修改稿时，就在投稿信里进行了说明，如下：

There is one thing I need to point out to you in particular. It's about Reviewer 2's comment on the data analysis method. This reviewer insisted that a paired-samples T-test should be performed instead of the independent-samples T-test, which is adopted in my paper. However, I think his/her suggestion may be wrong. As what I say in my response to this comment, the biggest difference between these two methods is that "an Independent T-Test is used to examine if there is a difference in the means of two DIFFERENT groups, while a Paired Samples T-Test is to test if there is a difference in the means between the members of only ONE group (in which The SAME participants are measured at different time intervals and compared; i. e. Time 1/ Time 2/ Time 3)". As my study is to "compare the means of two different groups (Group A and Group B), an independent-sample T-test is definitely more appropriate". In another comment made by the same reviewer, he/she suggested that I should update the section of Discussion after I have redone the data analysis using the paired-sampled T-test. I do not accommodate these two comments in my revised paper, since I think this reviewer might have misunderstood the two data analysis methods.

5) 实验描述方面的问题

此类问题包括实验对象的抽样、实验工具、实验步骤的介绍等。审稿人可能会对某些细节产生疑问，要求作者进一步解释。作者照做即可。

6) 讨论部分的问题

讨论部分是最容易被审稿人挑刺的地方，因为这一部分的写作涉及对数据的解读，对相关理论的应用，和前人研究的比较等方面。作者需要做的就是接受审稿人的建议或质疑，对该部分进行解释和修改。有时候，可能不太同意某些意见，那么就需要在回复时进行礼貌地解释，并且最好能引用他人的说法进行佐证。例如，笔者的一篇文章介绍了一种基于视频的匿名同伴互评的教学模式，可是审稿人认为既然人出现在视频中，就不可能是匿名的。对此，笔者引用了他人的研究对这一意见进行了礼貌的反驳和解释，如下：

Dear reviewer, I have to argue with you about what can be called "anonymous". According to scholars such as Lu and Bol (2007), "Anonymous peer review refers to a kind of peer review condition in which both reviewers and reviewees are kept unknown to one another", I do believe the peer review process involved in my experiment can be called "anonymous", since both reviewers and reviewees were kept unknown to each other in the experiment. Lin (2018), together with Marx (1999) considered anonymity as "a condition in which the real authors of communication units (e. g., messages) cannot be identified in terms of either their personal identities or their relevance in a social context", and I think the peer review process described in my paper also meets this standard.

According to your idea, a face and voice can be called identifiable information. Yes, faces and voices are identifiable information in some cases. However, the faces and voices helped nothing in identifying the feedback givers in the process described in my paper, since the participants were kept unknown to each other throughout the whole process. For the video feedback receivers, what they saw in the videos was simply a stranger saying or doing something. Generally speaking, there is no way (no need, either) for the video viewers to know the identity of the acting person in the video.

References:

Lin, G.-Y. (2018). Anonymous versus identified peer assessment via a Facebook-based learning application: Effects on quality of peer feedback, perceived learning, perceived fairness, and attitude toward the system. *Computers & Education*, 116, 81-92.

Lu, R., & Bol, L. (2007). A comparison of anonymous versus identifiable e-peer review on college student writing performance and the extent of critical feedback. *Journal of Interactive Online Learning*, 6(2), 100-115.

Marx, G. T. (1999). What's in a name? Some reflections on the sociology of anonymity *Information Society*, 15, 99-112.

这里要注意的是,在引用他人研究为自己辩护时,引用得越具体越好,附上原文的下载链接或至少给出原文的出版信息,以便审稿人进行比对。同时,这样做也能展示作者严谨的治学态度,从而给审稿人留下较好的印象。另外,有的作者可能担心反驳审稿人的意见会带来不好的结果,其实就笔者的经历而言,完全不必有此顾虑。只要做到有理有据,基本不会出现"反驳即失败"的情况。

7) 审稿人变卦情况的应对

有时候,审稿人在一审时并没有给出"拒稿"(reject)的意见,但在作者按照审稿意见修改后,复审时,该审稿人可能会突然给出"拒稿"的意见。对于这种情况,如果编辑给了我们再次修改的机会,那么在返回修改稿时,我们一定要在给编辑的回信(即 cover letter)中对该审稿人的拒稿意见进行详细申诉,并说明修改稿是如何处理这些拒稿意见的。

3.3 大修应对实例

下面以笔者的两篇有过大的修经历的论文为例,看看如何对审稿人和编辑的审稿意见作出回应。

实例 1(论文:Ge,2018)

这篇论文经历了一次大修和一次小修。首先来看大修修回时作者撰写的 Response to Reviewers' Comments 全文,供大家参考。

在修回信中,作者可以用不同颜色的文字分别表示审稿人的意见原文、作者对审稿人意见的回复,以及论文中修改的地方。此外,在修回信的开头,可以写一些客套话来表达对编辑给予自己修改机会的感谢和对审稿人的工作的感谢。

Dear Editor,

Thank you very much for your letter on May 7th, 2018 in regarding to my manuscript entitled "The impact of a forfeit-or-prize game-like teaching on e-learners' learning performance". I greatly appreciate the reviewers' and your efforts in handling my manuscript. Thank you for giving me the opportunity to revise my paper and I am also grateful to the reviewers' insightful comments.

I have carefully read the comments from the reviewers and revised the manuscript according to the suggestions. All these changes (including deletion) have been marked in red color in the revised manuscript. I hope this revision will make my manuscript more acceptable.

The responses to the reviewers' comments point by point are listed as below.

Please feel free to contact me with any questions and I am looking forward to your consideration.

Best regards,

Point-to-point responses to the comments:

Reviewer 1（审稿人1）

1) It seems that you could expand your keywords, as there are other terms and language found in your manuscript that could be included. Please consider revisiting your keywords to better develop terms that would help your manuscript be found by readers.

My response: I should say I totally agree with you on this point. The 5 keywords initially given were "game-based learning; reward strategy; e-learning; motivation; anxiety", but the journal has a requirement that "a maximum of 5 keywords should be chosen from the given list, which is printed in the Guide for Authors, and can also be found at the below site: http://www.elsevier.com/wps/find/journaldescription.cws_home/347/authorinstructions". That's why the current keywords were finally provided in my submitted manuscript. To be frank, the manuscript containing the original 6 keywords were returned to me for a revision in the technical check stage (part of the letter from the editorial office concerning the technical check is shown in the following figure). I have now replaced the current keywords with the original ones, and I hope it will be allowed by the journal at this stage.

```
Yours sincerely,
Administrative Support Agent
Administrative Support Agent [30-Mar-11]
Computers & Education

Comments:
1. A maximum of 5 keywords should be chosen from the given list, which is printed in the Guide for Authors, and can also be found at the
   below site:  http://www.elsevier.com/wps/find/journaldescription.cws_home/347/authorinstructions .
2. Pages should be numbered sequentially.
```

图 3-4　修回信中附图

分析：第一个问题，审稿人认为论文的关键词选得不好，建议作者修改关键词，使关键词更能表现出论文的研究内容，以便读者检索。在回复中，作者表达出完全同意审稿人的意见，并解释了当初选择这些关键词的原因——这份杂志要求作者在其关键词库中挑选关键词，否则不予送审。并且，作者在应答信中附上了杂志主页中对于关键词的说明截图（如图 3-4 所示）加以佐证。在回复的最后，作者说已经修改了关键词,希望可以得到杂志的允许。

2) You state that "educational games" are "also called serious games". Educational games and serious games are not necessarily the same thing. While many have made these terms synonymous, they are different forms of gaming with different intended purposes. Please consider revising this statement.

My response: Thanks for this comment, and I have dropped the term of "serious games" in the revised paper (fortunately, "serious games" only appear twice in the original manuscript), and only the term of "educational games" is kept in the paper now to make the paper more consistent in terminology and to eliminate possible misunderstanding among readers.

分析:第二个问题,审稿人认为文中不应该将 educational games 和 serious games 等同来用,认为两者的应用目标不同。作者回复:修改版中抛弃了 serious games,只用了 educational games,这样文中的术语会更具一致性,并且消除读者对术语可能产生的误解。

3) Between the statements, "In other words…" and "The present study tries…" I had hoped to see more rationale for why you are investigating rewards. You do a nice job of introducing video games in a general educational context, but don't speak to rewards at all. Please consider adding more of a transition from general educational games to rewards in the context of "more research of this kind is still needed to further our insights into the topic."

My response: Thanks for this comment! I have added more information as to why reward strategies need to be further explored in this part: One of the frequently examined elements in educational games is the reward, which is commonly perceived as a stimulus for game players. When a reward is involved in a game, the players generally will have more desire to win, and thus their motivation will be enhanced (Leftheriotis, Giannakos, & Jaccher, 2017). In educational settings, the most frequently adopted rewards include points, leaderboards, badges, etc. (Dicheva, Dichev, Agre, & Angelova, 2015). However, ~~due to the fact that~~ because the teaching and learning process is varied and changeable in different educational settings, there is no consensus on the concrete game forms or game designs in education (Hainey, et al., 2016; Tsai, Tsai, & Lin, 2015), and consequently, we cannot find consensus on reward strategies in educational games. In other words, more research ~~of this kind~~ is warranted ~~still needed~~ to enhance further our insights into the topic.

分析:第三个问题,审稿人认为作者应在文中进一步说明为何要研究奖惩策略在教育中的应用。审稿人还认为,作者在文献回顾中没有提及奖惩策略的问题,建议作者补充相关内容。作者在回复中表示完全同意这一意见,并在修改稿中对此类信息做了补充。

4) You state that "The present study tries to investigate…" Please consider the language, "The present study investigates…" Your manuscript either describes an investigation and makes a contribution, or it doesn't. (This comment also applies to the research questions section.)

You state that "… with the hope to shed some light…" Please consider the language, "… with the hope to shed light…"

My response:Thanks for this comment on language! I have revised these sentences according to this comment.

分析:这里,审稿人提出了写作的用词问题,作者在回信中表示接受。

5) You state that "… most of the studies were directed to the face-to-face classroom environment…" Please consider elaborating on this statement. I'm not sure what you mean and am afraid that other readers might also have questions.

My response:Thanks! I have added some information to explain this statement: The present study ~~tries to~~ investigates the impact of a forfeit-or-prize gamified teaching procedure in the an e-learning environment, with the intent hope to shed some light on the design of appropriate educational game forms for e-learners ~~in the e-learning environment~~. By examining the existing literature on the topic, we find that most of the empirical studies regarding reward strategies in gamified teaching and learning focus on traditional face-to-face classroom environment or take on-campus students as their target population. For example, of the 34 studies reviewed by Dicheva et al. (2015) on the topic of gamified teaching and learning, 25 studies were conducted in traditional classroom settings or took on-campus students as their subjects in the experiments. From this perspective, gamified teaching that focuses on e-learning scenarios is much in demand. This demand is also the focus of the present study. ~~which also makes the present study quite necessary~~.

分析:审稿人认为作者在文中说的"大多数此类研究都集中在面授的教学环境中"这一论断需要佐证,因为他/她不太清楚此论断的意思。作者在回信中表示修改稿中补充了对此疑问的说明信息,主要是列举了一个前人的研究来说明为何有此论断。

6) You state "It is exciting to see positive effects of educational games found in most of these empirical studies…". By "these empirical studies" do you mean

those cited? Or do you mean studies that have investigated games and learning in general? If the former, please consider the language "... found in most of these cited empirical studies..." If the latter, then I would disagree and would argue your statement is too bold. Instead, I would contend that the research is at best, mixed.

My response: Thanks! By saying "these empirical studies", I mean the studies reviewedin the paper. I have revised the sentence according to this comment: It is exciting to see positive effects of educational games found in most of these cited empirical studies...

分析：本条意见，审稿人针对文中语言表达提出疑问，置疑"in most of these empirical studies"中的"these empirical studies"到底指的是前文回顾的文章还是普通意义上针对游戏和学习进行研究的文章。审稿人认为，如果是前者的话，作者需要修改一下语言，将其变成"in most of these cited empirical studies"；而如果是后者的话，审稿人认为这条论断过于武断，他/她不赞成这一论断。作者回信中指出自己的意思是前者，并按照审稿人意见进行了修改。

7) You state that "This finding was overthrown..." Please consider another term instead of "overthrown". Perhaps "contradicted" might be better.

My response: Thanks! I have replaced "overthrown" with "contradicted".

分析：本条意见针对用词问题，毫无疑问，作者照单全收。

8) You state that "The game design and the reward strategies involved in the present study may shed some light on the application of gamification in the e-learning scenarios", but please also consider explaining why the study of reward systems is important toward this goal and who (what readers) will benefit the most from reading your manuscript.

My response: Thanks! The required information has been added in the revision: As discussed in the literature review in this article, various types of rewards often appear in educational games, and specific reward strategies sometimes produce a different impact on learners in the process of utilising games to learn something. It is necessary to probe into the question of how rewards can best elicit a desired outcome. In this sense, the game design and the reward strategies involved in the present study may shed ~~some~~ light on the application of gamification in the e-learning scenarios. The specific reward strategies adopted in the experiment may provide food for thought to teachers who want to apply games in their teaching practice.

分析：针对文中"本研究的游戏设计和奖励策略或许会对远程教学情境中的游

戏化教学做出解释"这句,审稿人认为作者应说明为何奖励策略如此重要,哪些读者会从本文获益。作者在回信中接受了意见,并在修改稿中对这两个问题做了说明。针对第一个问题,作者认为,前人的一些研究很多都对奖励策略进行了探讨,可见奖励策略的重要性。针对第二个问题,作者认为本文获益的读者群是想要进行游戏化教学的教师。

9) Please consider offering any other information you might have regarding the participants. For example, you state that "... we recruited 180 first-year adult e-learners..." How did you recruit these individuals?

My response: The required information has been added in the revision: The e-learning college mainly provides continuing education courses (a BS degree can be granted) to adult e-learners, and approximately 7,000 students will be newly enrolled in the college each school year. As a teacher at this college, the researcher of the present study is responsible for teaching several English courses. For the experiment, students enrolled in the course of College English Book Ⅱ (an obligatory course for first-year students) were taken as the target population, and the participants were randomly chosen from this population.

分析: 审稿人想知道作者是如何找到参与实验的180名学生的。在修改稿中,作者补充了相关解释,大意为:作者是一所网络教育机构的英语教师,学生众多,本实验的参与者选自于参加了大学英语课程的学员。

10) You state that "One month later, a delayed posttest... was administered to the three groups to determine whether there was any difference in knowledge retention between the three groups." Does this mean that the participants in the three groups weren't exposed to any other instruction or activities that help them reinforce what they learned or helped them retain the materials? I see that "The three Groups were not informed of the delayed posttest in advance, so as to minimize the influence of possible reviewing of the learning content by some participants." That's good, but do you know that they weren't exposed to further learning? If so, please consider stating this and how you know this. If not, please consider this a possible limitation that should be noted.

My response: Dear reviewer, I want to make some clarifications here. For the experiment described in my paper, there is completely no treatment to all of the three groups during the period between the posttest and the delayed posttest. It was assumed that "the participants in the three groups weren't exposed to any other instruction or activities that help them reinforce what they learned or helped them retain the materials" in this period, just as what you pointed out. What you are

worried about is the possibility that some students might do some reinforcing activities on their own. Yes, there is such possibility. However, according to many published papers (see studies by Hardiman, Rinne, & Yarmolinskaya, 2014; Mclaren, Adams, & Mayer, 2015; **Khoshsima, Saed & Yazdani**, 2015; Lee & Lyster, 2016) of the similar design of "a delayed posttest", there is no need to consider or state whether or not the subjects are doing any reinforcing activities on their own during this period (so long as there is no reinforcing treatment on them from the instructor), because this is hard to control (for example, some participants from any of the three groups might review the content at home), and even if some participants did do some reinforcing activities on their own, the possibility was the same for all the three groups.

References:

Mclaren, B. M., Adams, D. M., & Mayer, R. E. (2015). Delayed learning effects with erroneous examples: a study of learning decimals with a web-based tutor. *International Journal of Artificial Intelligence in Education*, 25(4), 520-542.

Hardiman, M., Rinne, L., & Yarmolinskaya, J. (2014). The effects of arts integration on long-term retention of academic content. *Mind, Brain & Education*, 8(3), 144-148.

Khoshsima, H., Saed, A., & Yazdani, A. (2015). Instructional Games and Vocabulary Enhancement: Case of Iranian Pre-Intermediate EFL Learners. *International Journal of Language and Linguistics*, 3(6), 328-332.

Lee, A. H., & Lyster, R. (2016). Effects of different types of corrective feedback on receptive skills in a second language: a speech perception training study. *Language Learning*, 66(4), 809-833.

分析:本条意见比较棘手,审稿人对于实验中的延迟后测(Delayed Posttest)的细节提出了疑问。审稿人置疑的是:从实验结束到一个月后进行的延迟后测期间,实验的参与者有没有接受一些其他的教学环节,从而帮助他们巩固前面学到的知识点。审稿人置疑作者到底知不知道学生有没有在延迟后测前进行了巩固学习。如果作者知道的话,审稿人要求作者在文章中说明这一点;如果作者不知道,审稿人希望作者将这一条列入本文的缺陷。对于这一审稿意见,作者在回信中做了详细说明,首先作者表示理解审稿人的这一疑虑;其次作者引用了前人已经发表的类似研究设计对于延迟后测进行了说明,大意是"实验结束到延迟后测的这一期间,学生到底有没有进行巩固学习,这很难被控制也很难让作者知悉,但是根据很多已经发表的论文中的延迟后测的设计来看,不太需要考虑参与者到底有没有进行了巩固学习,因为进行巩固学习的可能性对于参与实验的几个组来说是相同的。"

对于审稿人针对实验设计提出的置疑,作者在回信中一定要认真对待,最好能引经据典佐证自己的设计,否则万一出现回答不到位的地方,审稿人在复审时可能会作出"拒稿决定"。

11) Would the gamified materials be considered as part of your instrumentation? Did you build this gamified database material for this investigation? Please consider addressing these questions.

My response:Thanks for this comment. As I have stated in the paper, the gamified materials are actually online multiple-choice question quizzes, which are very common for e-learning education. The quiz game described in the paper was carried out with the use of a free software called Rain Classroom (available at http://ykt.io/). Hence, there is no specially designed gamified database for this investigation. I have added some information about Rain Classroom to make readers better understand the gamified learning process: When a participant had ~~made his or her mind about~~ decided on the difficulty level, a question of the desired difficulty level would be retrieved from the database and would be shown through the interface of a free software called Rain Classroom (available at http://ykt.io/) on every participants' screen (see Fig. 1).

分析:审稿人想知道实验中的游戏化的教学材料是否应被看作实验工具的一部分,还想知道实验中用到的游戏化数据库是否是作者自己建造的,审稿人希望作者可以在文中对这些做以说明。对于这种要求,作者自然应该全盘接受并在修改稿中加以说明。作者在回信中解释:实验中使用的游戏化教材其实就是在线选择题而已,这些材料对于远程教学机构来说很普通,而本次实验中使用的游戏化平台其实是一个免费的在线教学工具"雨课堂"(Rain Classroom),并给出了该工具的在线网址。

12) You state that "This result means that the forfeit-or-prize reward pattern was the best…" Please consider changing "means" to "suggests" as to use more careful language in making conclusions about your findings.

My response:Thanks for this comment. I have changed the wording according to your comment.

分析:审稿人对于用词进行了建议,认为原文的"means(意味着)"应该改成"suggests(暗示)",认为"suggest"在表达论断时比"mean"更保守。这种意见一般都是直接接受即可。

13) You state that "The results of the present study indicate that…".

Again, consider the word "suggest" instead of "indicate".

My response: Thank you! I have changed the wording according to your comment.

分析：此条意见和上面一条一样，审稿人认为作者应该用"suggest"代替原文中的"indicate"，原因同上。

14) You state that "... that the present study has verified the effectiveness of game-based learning ... ". Again, consider more careful language. For example, "... that the present study has offered evidence for the effectiveness of game-based learning ... "

You state that "... present study is obviously much easier ... " Again, consider more careful language. For example, "... present study is much easier ... "

My response: Thanks again. These two sentences have been revised according to your comment.

分析：此条意见和上面一样，审稿人认为作者应该用更为保守的语言，不要在下论断时用过于肯定的词语。作者同样接受此意见。

15) How do your findings make a unique contribution to the area of study on video games and learning? That is, what does your investigation reveal that hasn't already been offered? Please consider speaking to these questions in your discussion or subsequent conclusion.

My response: Thanks for this comment. First, I have to say that the game described in my paper is just a quiz game in nature. The quiz game can be carried out over the Internet or with just paper and pen. From this perspective, it is not a video game in the common sense. However, to accommodate this comment, I have added more information in Discussion and Conclusion to say more about the unique contribution of my study to the existing literature: The game forms adopted in the present study may provide some food for thought when we design educational games to be used in specific educational scenarios for educating specific population. With the development of various types of educational technologies, many educators like to accommodate the latest technologies in gamified teaching (such as Augmented Reality or Virtual Reality). From this perspective, the technologies adopted in the present study are nothing new (only computers, headphones, a quiz software were used). However, the carefully designed gaming strategies might have offset the lack of advanced technologies for the effectiveness of the teaching process. The strategies described in the present study are easy to be implemented over the Internet for educating adult e-leaners.

In this sense, when we design educational games, we should probably focus more on gaming strategies rather than on the latest or the most advanced technology.

...

The gaming strategies adopted in the present study have been proved to be easy to implement and successful in generating effective learning performance, which suggests that educational game developers and designers should focus more on gaming strategies rather than on the latest or the most advanced technologies.

分析:这条意见涉及讨论和结论部分,回复此类意见时要十分谨慎。审稿人提出作者应该在讨论和结论部分对本文的创新点进行更详细的说明。对于这种意见,我们是一定要接受的。很多作者对自己文章的创新点不太自信,在文章中不太敢仔细分析,所以有的审稿人抓住这一点,如果作者对此给不出很好的解释,可能会被拒稿,所以一定要按照意见进行补充。正如"世界上没有完全相同的两片树叶",我们的研究也是如此,所以只要仔细分析,总能找出自己文章和前人文章的不同,然后对这些不同点进行深入分析即可形成自己文章的创新点了。针对此意见,笔者在修改稿中这样介绍创新点:虽然已有很多文章应用了各种各样的游戏化技术于教学中,但是本文的实验着重描写的是设计巧妙而又容易操作的游戏化策略,而非游戏技术。从这种意义上来说,所谓的游戏化教学可能并非要将重点放在游戏技术上,而是应该放在游戏策略上。

16) Overall, the manuscript is well written and clearly articulated. I have one main sticking point that I feel needs to be further fleshed out. You do a good job of introducing educational gaming in general, but then immediately jump into the investigation of rewards. I feel you need more of a transition between this general discussion and that of reward. You do go into reward in your literature review. Again, working from general to specific. But feel that you need to offer more within your introduction.

My response:Thanks! **In my understanding, this comment is the same as or similar to Comment #3 mentioned earlier in this response letter. I have added some transitional information in Introduction of this paper, as indicated in my response to Comment #3.**

分析:审稿人认为作者在文中对于游戏化教学和游戏化教学中的奖惩策略都介绍得挺好,但是两者之间缺少过渡和衔接,认为作者应在文章的第一部分(即 Introduction 部分)进一步说明两者的关系。作者在回信中认为此条意见和前面的第三条意见基本一样,所以在根据第三条意见修改论文后,本条意见也得以解决。

17) Finally, please consider having the manuscript professionally edited for

clarity and grammar. For example: Please consider checking with the journal to see if "180 participants were recruited…" should not start with a number, but rather, the number should be spelled out. That is "One hundred and eighty participants were recruited…" Consider checking the journal for consistency of language and spellings. For example, "forfeit-or prize" is also found as "forfeit-or-prize". "the pretest was employed…" should be "The pretest was employed…"

My response: Thank you again for reviewing my paper. I have now completed another round of proofreading of my manuscript to accommodate the comments you mentioned here. Besides, I have used the service of an international language editing company named "AJE" (see the editorial certificate provided by this company in the following figure) to further edit my paper for clarity and grammar.

分析：最后，审稿人希望作者可以找专业人士对文章进行润色（表达和语法），并列举了一些遣词造句上的问题。对于这种意见，我们一般有两种解决办法：一是自己或请朋友对文章进行仔细校正，二是找专业润色机构来做。本文作者由于时间方面的原因找了润色机构来进行校对工作，并附上了该机构发布的校对证书。一般来说，找业内有名的润色机构比较省事，修回时也更有底气。当然，找润色机构需要支付一定的润色费。需要指出的是，润色机构对论文进行润色后，作者一定要通读一遍，以防其润色时有所不当。

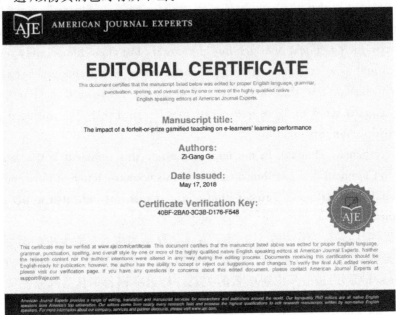

图 3-5　修回信中出示论文润色的证据

Reviewer 2 (审稿人 2):

1) My reservation with the paper is more semantic than the quality of the methodology, analysis and recommendations and can be addressed. The paper would benefit greatly from an edit by a native English speaker semantically the paper is confusing and the English has some rudimentary error that could be addressed through native editing.

The data collected and analysis is robust and scientifically valid and general layout of the paper is very good. My recommendation is to revise with modification and semantic clarity.

My response:Thank you your effort in reviewing my paper. To tackle the language problem of my paper, I have used the service of an international language editing company named "AJE" (see the editorial certificate provided by this company in the following figure) to further edit my paper for clarity and grammar.

(注:润色证据见图 3-5)

分析:第二位审稿人也认为文章需要润色。作者在修回时附上了润色证据。

2) My other reservation is the use of the descriptor "game like". On the evidence of the paper there is little gameplay in the activities, quizzes and reward processes yes but the pedagogic activity consists of testing or assessment of one variety or another with extrinsic motivational rewards. The author should re think the descriptions of activities in this context though I am uncomfortable with the term "gamification" the term might be more fitting to this particular pedagogic activity.

My response:Thanks again. The reason why I used "game like" is just like what you pointed out here. Quizzes are pure assessments or the so-called quiz games? I was not quite certain when I wrote the paper, because educators may have different opinions toward them. However, as there are some kinds of rewards and different reward patterns involved in the teaching and learning process, I believe the quiz form applied in the present study may acquire some elements of educational games. for the revised version of the paper, I have used "gamified" to replace "game like", as the former is more widely used in the existing literature, just as you pointed out.

分析:审稿人对于文中的"game like"提出质疑,认为文中描述的教学活动(测验形式)没有什么游戏因素。对此,作者在回信中进行了解释,作者认为测验可以具有游戏化的形式,因为其中涉及一些奖惩策略,这些策略也经常出现在游戏中。不过,鉴于审稿人提出了质疑,作者在修改稿中用"gamified"代替了"game like",

因为前者更常用。

3) There is little or no evidence of playfulness in the activity (which I understand is very complex to frame, measure and analyse) therefore the methodology whilst sound, scientifically robust provides us with little new knowledge suffice as to say in assessment rewards combined with forfeits benefit e learning assessment in this context.

My response: As I have explained in my response to your Comment #2, different people may have different ideas as to whether quizzes are games or not, it is also true with the so-called "playfulness" in the activity. Moreover, the theoretical and pedagogical implications mentioned in Discussion, I believe, do provide something new to the existing literature (such as the description of the interrelationship between motivation and anxiety). Moreover, I have now added a paragraph in Discussion to further state the unique contribution of my study to the existing literature: The game form adopted in the present study may provide food for thought when we design educational games to be used in specific educational scenarios for educating specific populations. With the development of various types of educational technologies, more educators opt to accommodate the latest technologies in gamified teaching (such as augmented reality or virtual reality). Compared with these technologies, the technologies adopted in the present study are old-fashioned (only computers, headphones, and a quiz software were used). However, the carefully designed gaming strategies might have offset the lack of advanced technologies for the effectiveness of the teaching process. The strategies for educating adult e-learners, described in the present study, are easily implemented on the Internet. In this sense, it might suggest that we should focus more on gaming strategies rather than on the latest or the most advanced technology when we design educational games.

分析: 审稿人认为文中描述的教学活动没有游戏性，这样一来，很难说奖惩结合的教学方法会对远程学习产生益处。这一条意见非常负面，如果回答得不好，很可能被拒稿。对此，作者在回信中进行了辩解，大意为：每个人对于哪种教学形式属于游戏化教学是有不同理解的，同样，每个人对于教学活动中有没有游戏性也会有不同的看法。接下来，作者进一步指出文章的讨论部分对本研究的创新点做了深入的探讨，特别是在讨论部分新增了一段内容指出本研究虽然没有用新奇的技术手段，但是胜在奖惩策略的应用上既有效又容易操作。

大修返回后，经过二次审稿，编辑又给了一次小修的机会，我们来看看小修的回复信。从下面的回复信可以看出，小修和大修的修回信格式基本一致。小修时，对于文中的变动,作者用了紫色的字体来标注。此外,从回复中,我们只看到了一位审稿人提了意见,这表明在二审时,编辑只将修改稿送给了一位审稿人进行二审。此外,我们从小修回信中也可以看到,由于一修时进行了仔细修改,二修时审稿人并没有提出需要大动干戈的修改意见,多是词句方面的小建议。

Dear Editor,

  Thank you very much for giving me another chance to revise my paper entitled "The impact of a forfeit-or-prize gamified teaching on e-learners' learning performance".

  The responses to your and the reviewers' comments point by point are listed as below. I have carefully read the comments and tried my best to accommodate them into the second revision. The changes are marked in purple color in the latest revision. Please feel free to contact me with any questions and I am looking forward to your consideration.

Point-to-point responses to the comments:

  Editor's comment: Please try your best to show the significance or academic contribution of your paper. Adding more discussion or implications may be one way of improving this.

  My response: I have added more in the section of discussion to strengthen the academic contribution of my study, and I hope this version will be better:

  Taken together, the results of the present study reveal the necessity of balancing between rewards and learning anxiety (pressure or stress or competition) in teaching and learning. As mentioned above, both rewards and anxiety can impact learning motivation. To some extent, reward and anxiety often go side by side. When a reward is set for a certain task, anxiety is naturally induced when people compete for that reward. Moreover, the levels of anxiety can be adjusted by the design of reward strategies. This assertion can be exemplified by the results of applying different reward strategies to Group A and Group B, where the forfeit-or-prize reward strategy utilized by Group A induced more learning anxiety than the prize-only strategy used by Group B. However, few studies have explored learning motivation from perspectives of both rewards and learning pressure, not to mention how to incorporate them in teaching and learning (Dicheva et al., 2015). This deficiency has been made up for by the present study, which examined the impact of game-based learning on learning performance by taking both rewards and learning anxiety into exploration.

...

Moreover, when we design reward strategies, we need consider game forms and target populations. Take the present study as an example: the game form was an online multiple-choice quiz game and the target population included only adult learners. With these in mind, we finally took grade scores as the reward in the gamified learning process, because the most common reward for multiple-choice quizzes is the quiz score, and what these adult learners concerned most was their course grade. We intentionally linked the quiz score with the course grade, so that the gamified process could generate desired impact on learning performance.

分析：此次小修，负责此论文的编辑也提出了意见，大致意思是让作者尽可能地突出本文的创新点和对此类研究的学术贡献，并建议作者对此增加一些讨论内容或多写一些本文的意义（一般包括理论意义（Theoretical Implication）和实践意义（Practical Implication））。这些内容一般都出现在文章的讨论部分（Discussion）。作者在回复中感谢了编辑，并在修改稿中增加了相应的内容。

Reviewer 1（审稿人1）：

1) LITERATURE REVIEW

"Educational games have been used for teaching language … medicine (Greer et al., 2016), etc." Please consider not using "etc.". Rather consider, "For instance, educational games have been used … , and medicine (Greer et al., 2016)."

My response：Thanks. I have changed the wording according to your suggestion.

分析：此次的审稿人（是否为一审中的审稿人未知）按照文章的章节给出了意见。本条意见针对论文的文献回顾部分，审稿人提出不要用"etc."的字眼。对于这种用词建议，我们一般接受即可。

2) METHODS

Participants

"The participants' consent was obtained via email before commencement of the experiment." Please consider moving this sentence into the Procedure section.

My response：Thank you! I have done so as you suggested.

分析：本条意见针对论文的实验方法部分，审稿人提出句子变动的建议。对于这种用词建议，我们接受即可。

3) Instruments

"As the first-year e-learners, these participants were enrolled to learn College English Book Ⅱ issued by Shanghai Foreign Language Education Press." You mentioned College English Book Ⅱ in the participants section as well. Do you need this sentence?

My response：Thanks! I have deleted the sentence.

分析：本条意见针对实验方法部分中的实验工具小节，审稿人提出句子变动的建议。对于这种用词建议，我们接受即可。

4) RESULTS

Results of the two questionnaires

What was the two questionnaires based on? Perhaps I missed it. But did you base the questions on existing instruments that have shown reliability/validity? I see you state the reliability, but did you create these instruments? Please consider speaking to this in the instruments section.

My response：Thanks! The two questionnaires were newly developed by us, and I have now added such information in the section of Results：

Both questionnaires were newly developed by us for the present study.

分析：本条意见针对论文的实验结果部分，审稿人对于文章中使用的两个量表提出疑问，他/她想知道这两个量表是用的前人设计的现成量表还是作者自己编制的。在回信中，作者做了解释，并在修改稿中补充了有关量表的信息。

5) DISCUSSION

"Compared with these technologies, the technologies adopted in the present study are old-fashioned…" Please consider another word than "old-fashioned". Perhaps "Compared with these technologies, the technologies adopted in the present study could be perceived as commonplace…"?

My response：Thanks! I have changed the wording according to your suggestion.

分析：本条意见针对论文的讨论部分，审稿人提出用词的建议。对于这种用词建议，一般我们接受即可。

6) CONCLUSION

"The gaming strategies adopted in the present study have been proved…" Please consider not using "proved". Rather consider, "The gaming strategies adopted in the present study are not only easy to implement but may also be successful in …".

My response：Thanks! I have rewritten the sentence according to this comment.

分析：本条意见针对论文的结论部分，审稿人提出句子变动的建议。对于这种建议，我们接受即可。

7) REFERENCES

"References" shows up twice.

My response：Thank you very much! I have deleted one of them.

分析：本条意见针对论文的参考文献部分，审稿人指出了一些校对上的问题。对于这种建议，我们接受即可。

实例 2（论文：Ge，2019）

Dear editor and reviewers,

I have carefully read the comments from you and revised the manuscript according to your suggestions. Besides, I have also finished another round of proofreading of my manuscript to further edit my paper for clarity and grammar. All the changes (including deletion) have been marked in red color this time in the revised manuscript. I hope the revision will make my manuscript more acceptable.

分析：作者在回信中首先感谢了编辑和审稿人给予修改的机会，然后表示自己对论文的语言和语法进行了修改。

Editor's Comments：

Section 5 could usefully be summarised in a table but please bear in mind the reviewer comments concerning the number of tables when considering your revision.

My response：Thanks! I have made some changes in section 5 concerning the tables. The original Table 4 (Tests of between-subjects effects) is deleted, since the description of this test in the manuscript is enough for readers' understanding. Besides, the original Table 8 is moved to the end of the paper as Appendix B.

分析：这是编辑给出的一条意见，编辑认为文章的第 5 部分可以用一个表格进行归纳，但同时又提醒作者也要注意审稿人的意见之一——文中的表格数量较多。作者在回信中说修改稿删去了 Table 4，因为文中的叙述已经可以体现出 Table 4 的含义了。此外，将 Table 8 移至文末作为附录。

Reviewer 1（审稿人 1）：

1) First, the manuscript the designed experimental study, in my view, conflates an effort to reduce potential bias, with a well-designed study. As can be

seen in my following comments, there are challenges with the study that handicap its outcomes. The research questions are poorly worded (this may be due to translation), and more in the form (the first 3) of expecting a yes, no answer. The fourth research question is not well-connected to the first three questions.

My response: Thanks for your effort in reviewing my paper. I am confused for this comment, because there are only 3 research questions listed in my paper, and the fourth research question you mentioned does not exist at all. So far as the three research questions are concerned, the first two are related to the qualitative research design and hence a yes-no answer is normally desired. The third question is related to the questionnaire survey and the semi-structured interview. On the whole, the three questions are related to the topic of paper, that is learning media type and learning media preference. As you commented that the research questions are poorly worded, I have now revised the three questions, and I hope this version will be better:

A) Is there any significant difference between the six groups in their learning outcomes ~~Can significant differences be found in learning outcomes among the six groups~~?

B) Does the mismatch between learners' media preference and the assigned media bring a learning failure ~~negatively influence their learning~~?

C) What are the perceptions of ~~do~~ the e-learners ~~have~~ towards the learning media they are assigned?

分析：审稿人的第一条意见比较尖锐，他/她认为实验的设计可能存在缺陷，文中描述的研究问题用词不当，这些研究问题多期待"是与否(Yes or No)"的答案，而且第4个研究问题和前3个研究问题不太相关。作者在回信中并没有对实验的设计做出回应，因为此条意见中也并没有指出实验设计的哪个方面存在问题。作者主要对审稿人对于研究问题的质疑做了解释。作者认为研究问题1、研究问题2与本实验的定量研究属性相关，一般研究问题的表现形式确实多用这种"Yes or No"的答案，而研究问题3与实验中的问卷和访谈相关。而且总体来看，这三个研究问题都和本文讨论的主题相关，即学习媒体的类型和对学习媒体的偏好。而审稿人提出的研究问题4根本没有出现在文章中，这表明审稿人审稿有误(作者在应答信中并没有直白地说审稿人错了，而是指出问题4并没有出现在文章中，这样审稿人的该条意见可以忽略)。由于审稿人认为研究问题的遣词造句比较差，作者在回复中表示修改稿对此部分进行了修改。

2) The survey/questionnaire, which was adapted, was poorly worded, confusing, and I simply can't see how the researchers would have received useful

data from the survey (see Appendix A). For example, there is a question about understanding content better from a lecture. But, there is a closely followed question that asks about learning better from listening. It is not clear how these are distinctly different, and as such, how the responses can be easily and accurately interpreted.

My response：Dear reviewer, the wording of the adapted questionnaire (Questionnaire A) is almost completely the same as that of the original version of "Perceptual Learning Style Preference Questionnaire" developed by Joy Reid" (1984), and the change in wording was slight and trivial; for example, my version replaced "chalkboard" in the original version with "screen", because the teaching process described in my paper was carried out online with computers and the Internet as the teaching tools, which is different from the traditional classroom teaching described in the original version of Joy Reid. Another difference is that my version has dropped many items in the original. In addition, you mentioned that the order of the items confused you, but actually I have made some explanation in my paper about the order of the items ("the items in the questionnaire were shuffled to avoid possible side effects"). All in all, my version is almost the same as the original in wording. I don't know why you think the adapted version was poorly worded. The original version has been used by numerous researchers over the world. For your convenience, you can find the original version at：http://www.doc88.com/p-074650289479.html. May I ask you to kindly have a look at the original version? If you compare the original with mine, you will find the wording of the two versions is almost the same. I have added more information about the differences between my version and the original version in the revised manuscript.

分析：从这条意见来看，此审稿人似乎对相关研究了解不多，审稿人认为文中使用的量表表述不清。作者在回信中进行了反驳：首先，这个量表并非作者自己完全重新编制的，而是在前人编制的量表上稍做修改，而且这个量表已经被众多研究所采用，编制者的母语也是英语，不存在用词表述不清的问题，并给出了原量表的来源和在线浏览地址；其次，作者详细解释了实验所用量表和原量表的不同之处，可以看出不同点很少。在此基础上，作者质疑为何审稿人认为量表表述不清，并恳请该审稿人看看原量表（反驳时，语言表述上尽量礼貌，不要冷嘲热讽）。从这一条意见的回应可以看出，有时候审稿人也未必很专业很认真地审稿，所以在有理有据的情况下，我们对错误的审稿意见完全可以据理力争。在返回修改稿的时候，我们可以在 Cover Letter 中向编辑说明这些情况。

3) Finally, assumptions and claims are made throughout, that seem problematic, and certainly unsupported. For example, in the methods section, the authors claim that harder problems will reveal more about whether the students do better using one learning form, or another. In short, while I found the topic to be interesting, I do not suggest that the manuscript be moved forward at this time.

My response: Dear reviewer, thanks again for your efforts in reviewing my paper. I have reexamined the paper and revised assumptions and claims (some supporting information is provided now) to accommodate this comment.

For example:

Moreover, according to Ge (2015), the proficiency level of most Chinese non-English major adult e-leaners was quite low, so the on-screen text, the audios, and the videos used in the present study were mostly constructed in Chinese with illustrations of English sentences.

Another example:

It is obvious from *Table* 2 that all the six groups were very weak at their prior knowledge of English gerund (all the means of the six groups were less than two points), and there was no statistical difference ($F(5, 208)=1.873$, P value $=0.100 > 0.05$) in the pretest between the groups.

分析：从这条审稿意见来看，这名审稿人其实就是做了"拒稿"的判定，他/她认为，虽然该文研究话题很有趣，但是不应再往下走流程了（Move Forward）。对于这种审稿人拒稿，但是编辑又给了修改机会的情况，作者心理要清楚其实编辑对文章是感兴趣的，不然也不会给予修改的机会。反过来看，这条意见的大意是作者在文中做了很多没有证据的判断和猜想。作者在回信中表示已经采纳这条意见，在修改稿中对下论断的地方补充了支持信息。这里要提醒大家的是，对于这种比较笼统的意见，我们不需要反驳，只需要在修改稿中按要求做一些修改即可。

Reviewer 2（审稿人2）：

1) Overall, this paper deals with a topic which has not been investigated in this way, yet. Furthermore, it seems in some ways interesting that there is almost no effect of media preference combined with used media on academic performance. But the question is anyhow, whether this research is necessary as there exist a myth of learning styles (see Kirschner, P. (2017). Stop propagating the learning styles myth, Computers & Education, 106, 166-171). But the authors speak about media preferences which seems to be better. On the other hand, the questionnaire in Appendix A is an adaption of the "Perceptual

Learning Style Preference Questionnaire"! Eventually, the authors may include the above-mentioned article in their manuscript in order to face possible critique that there are no media preferences.

My response：Dear reviewer, thanks for your detailed comments on my manuscript. I have cited the paper of Kirschner (2017) in my paper as you suggested：

However, scholars such as Kirschner (2017) holds a disapproving attitude towards the notion of learning styles, and he claimed that we should stop propagating the learning styles myth, because there is no way to classify learners into distinct groups of learning styles. Whether learning styles can be determined is still worth discussing, but the claim made by Kirshner (2017) that "what people prefer is not, per definition, what is best for them" obviously calls for the topic of the present study, which is about the impact of media preference and learners' received media on learning performance.

分析：审稿人 2 的第一条意见也颇为尖锐，他/她指出有学者（Kirschner，2017）认为可能根本就没有所谓的学习风格（Learning Styles）一说（Kirschner 认为根本不可能将学习者划分为清晰的学习风格类型），所以本研究是否有必要也有待商榷，但是因为本文用的是媒体偏好（Media Preference）而非学习风格，所以避开了学习风格是否存在的话题。该审稿人建议作者在文中引用 Kirschner 发表于 2017 年的这篇文章。作者在回复中表示会引用此文献，并在修改稿中对此问题进行了相应地说明。

2) What I miss in the paper is the focus on the issue that audio and text are compared with each other in this study. Even though, the authors report a lot of studies, the focus is more on videos and animations. I think, the manuscript will profit from a more specified presentation of studies in respect of the topic of the manuscript. The authors should also precise why this study is necessary, and which gap they fill in research. The research must be better justified. This issue is strongly connected to the article of Kirschner (2017).

My response：Thanks! I have now added more about audio and text in Section 2，**and also argued more for the necessity of the present study；for example**：

Text, whether visual or spoken (audio), is one of the most traditional learning media, and much research has been done about the optimization of using text in educational practice. Some studies compared the impact of visual text on learning performance with that of audio text. For example, the study by Gerjets, Rummer, Scheiter, and Schweppe (2008) compared auditory text materials and visual text materials and found that it was easier for learners to retain an auditory list than a visual one, because auditory-sensory representations were assumed "to be more durable than visual-sensory representations". This finding finds support from the study carried out by de Oliveira Neto, Huang, and Melli (2015), in which 91 participants enrolled for an online technical course were divided into an audio learning material group (46 learners) and a visual text learning material group (45 learners). This study found that the audio group responded more efficiently to the transfer test than the text group. The researchers tried to explain the result by applying the cognitive load theory and they claimed that the learners in the text group perceived a higher cognitive load than those in the audio group. In addition to such kind of one-to-one comparison research design, other studies tried to probe text with a more complicated research design. A case in point is the study by Kim and Gilman (2008), which found that the Korean learners would learn English vocabulary better in two conditions: 1) visual text combined with graphics or 2) visual text combined with spoken text and graphics; however, learners achieved less when they were provided visual text or spoken text alone. The likely reason they provided is that graphics allow learners to visualize the definition of words in a more meaningful way.

...

All in all, as indicated by some scholars, there is not enough empirical research on the justification of applying learning-styles assessment (including media preference assessment) in general educational practice (Kirschner 2017; Pashler, McDaniel, Rohrer, and Bjork, 2009), and there is lacking empirical effort to study the effect of various media types on adult learners in online education (de Oliveira Neto, Huang, and Melli, 2015). Moreover, there is seldom any study in the existing literature that is designed to explore whether there is any impact on learning outcomes brought about by the crossover manipulation of different learning media regarding learners' different media preferences. The present study, which took media preferences as its focus and was set in an e-learning environment, has the potential to meet the call for the study of learning styles' impact on e-learners' learning performance from the aspect of media preferences.

分析：审稿人认为文章对于音频和文本这两种学习媒体介绍不足，而过多地谈论视频和动画，审稿人建议作者补充一些关于音频和文本学习媒体的内容。同时，审稿人希望作者可以突出本研究的意义，并再次提醒作者本研究和 Kirschner

(2017)的研究有联系。作者在回信中表明修改稿增加了有关音频和文本的内容，对本文的创新点做了补充，并引用了 Kirschner(2017)的文献。

3) Abstract：The last sentence, "Possible explanations to the findings are discussed", is saying almost nothing. I would prefer one main conclusion regarding the study. By the way：What is the main conclusion of the study? This is missing in the text!

My response：Thank you! I have now deleted the last sentence, and revised some sentences in the Abstract to show the main finding of the study：

The study concludes that learners' personal media preference, though effected some impact on learning, did not lead to significant differences on learners if they were provided with the same type of learning media; however, if different learning media were assigned to learners with the same media preference, significant differences in learning outcome can be found. Another finding is ~~The results showed~~ that the combined media has the most positive impact on the participants' autonomous learning ~~was the most effective learning media, and the mismatch between media preference and media assigned did not cause expected learning failure~~.

分析：审稿人认为摘要中的最后一句"文章讨论了可以解释实验发现的相关内容"毫无意义，他认为摘要中应给出研究的总体结论，而此摘要中并没有提及。作者在回复中表示按照此条意见修改了论文的摘要部分。

4) Introduction：The introduction starts with multimedia environments and the kind how information processing takes place in human beings according to the Cognitive Theory of Multimedia Learning or Paivio's Dual Coding Theory or Sweller's Cognitive Load Theory. These theories are empirically already investigated showing that learners show best performance when receiving information using two senses, most often the visual and the auditory sense. Results of these studies are missing. Even though, these studies did not consider diverse media preferences, results may also be used to assume that providing two media may show best results in performance.

My response：Thank you for this detailed comment. I have now accommodated your view in the revised version and the necessity for the present study is also further emphasized：

All these theories have uncovered the complexity of multimedia learning, and they generally show that learners tend to perform better when receiving information based on two senses (most often the visual and the auditory sense).

However, empirical studies employing these theories were normally carried out in traditional classroom teaching and learning practice but not the e-learning environment, and these studies did not consider diverse media preferences in their exploration (Mayer, 2017). The present study may hopefully provide more empirical evidences to remedy the gap.

分析：审稿人认为虽然文章在前言部分（Introduction）提及的多媒体认知理论、Paivio 的双重编码理论和 Sweller 的认知负荷理论没有考虑媒体偏好的问题，但是已有实验证明了学习者采用两种感官获取信息会得到较好的学习效果。审稿人认为，本研究在该部分没有介绍此类已有的发现，希望作者可以补充此类信息，从而用这些信息佐证使用两种学习媒体或许可以在学习中有更好的效果。作者对此表示接受，并在修改稿中补充了相关信息。

5) Literature Review: The literature review is subdivided into two sub-headings with 2.1. Learning Media and 2.2. Learning Media Preferences. Regarding learning media, the authors describe in the second paragraph results on the comparison between animations and static texts or pictures, even though, in their study animations are not used. Furthermore, in the third paragraph they show studies on videos - again these are not used in their study. It would be better to concentrate on the comparison which is necessary for the study. These results could also not explain the own study results. Eventually, these two paragraphs could be strengthened a little bit in order to focus on the objective of the own study conducted.

Instead of reporting results, the authors may also refer to the theoretical assumptions how diverse media is cognitively processed. Overall, this section could be strengthened and focused on the own research. Regarding learning media preferences, the article of Kirschner (2017) should be considered, mentioned, and discussed.

My response: Thanks! I think this comment is similar to Comment #1 and #2. I have revised the part accordingly. I did not delete the review on animation or video because animation and video are among the most frequently used media types in educational practice, but I added a paragraph about audio and text, which is more related to the experiment described in the present study. In addition, I have added some information about the comparison between animation and audio, and also that between video and audio. Moreover, the work by Kirschner (2017) is also cited and discussed in the revised version. Here are some examples of the revision:

As Mayer (2003) once claimed in his article that the prospect of multimedia learning lies in the hope that students can learn more deeply from messages involving words and pictures than from those based on words alone. However, no one knows for sure how diverse media are cognitively processed in the learning process, though some theories concerning the cognitive process of multimedia learning have been proposed by scholars, such as Mayer's Cognitive Theory of Multimedia Learning (2002), Paivio's Dual-Coding theory (1986), and Swellers' Cognitive Load theory (2010), which have been mentioned in the Introduction section of the present paper.

...

Video materials have also been compared with audio-only ones; for example, Baggett (1984) found that video materials are more capable of eliciting long-term retention span in learners than the audio-only version. Scholars such as Baggett (*ibid.*) believe that a critical attribute of video to learning lies in its ability to use both auditory and visual symbol systems, and when audio and visual information is combined into a video, each source will provide additional and complementary information.

分析：审稿人认为在文章的文献回顾部分，作者回顾了有关动画、视频学习媒体的内容，而这两种媒体形式并没有出现在论文的实验中。审稿人建议作者应多回顾和本研究相关的学习媒体，如音频和文本媒体。此外，审稿人还指出在文献回顾部分，作者应该补充有关不同媒体形式在认知处理方面的话题，从而加强文献回顾的深度，同时再次指出作者应引用并分析 Kirschner(2017)的文章。在回复中，作者完全接受此意见，并指出这条意见和前面的第一、二条意见相似，并解释说在修改稿中并没有删除有关动画、视频媒体的信息，因为这两种媒体形式是学习媒体中频繁使用的两种形式，但是修改稿增加了有关音频和文本媒体的内容。

6) Research Questions: In the research questions, the authors discuss the issue on validating experiments. I think this is superfluous as the principles of an experiment are clear to any reader. Furthermore, this would be an aspect which could be discussed in the method section. I think, the most important point is that the study is a field experiment with a random assignment of the participants to six experimental groups.

My response: Thank you! I have now deleted the information on validating experiments in this section as you advised.

分析：审稿人认为在研究问题部分，作者没有必要介绍一些实验的规则，因为读者都清楚这些规则。此外，这些规则如果要介绍也应放在文章的研究方法部分(Method)。作者在回信中表示接受这条意见，并在修改稿中删除了相应的信息。

7) Method: The heading "instruments" does not exactly fit to the text. In my point of view, the authors describe only in the beginning the materials used for the experiment. But then, they describe the six diverse experimental conditions. Thus, I would name the heading "Experimental Conditions" or "Experimental Groups". You could also make a sub-heading about "Learning Content". Shortly, the pre-test is mentioned in the next paragraph. What I miss is a subheading with e. g. "Data Sources". In this passage, not only the pre- and post-test should be mentioned. When I see it correctly, the post-test issues are missing, too.

Furthermore, the questionnaire concerning learners' perceptions of the learning media is just as missing as the semi-structured interview which was conducted after the study with 10 participants. It is also not mentioned how many participants were asked with the semi-structured interview per condition. In which condition were two persons asked and why?

My response: Thanks! I have changed the heading from "instruments" to "Learning Content", and a subsection named "Data Sources" has been added as well, in which information about the posttest, the questionnaire, the semi-structured interview is provided (besides, the semi-structured interview was carried out for 60 participants, and my original words in the manuscript are "we only randomly selected ten participants from each of the six groups", which might have caused some misunderstanding. Sorry about this, and I have revised the sentences to make the description clearer):

4.3 *Data Sources*

The participants would have one week to digest the learning materials assigned to them, and then they would receive an online posttest. The posttest underwent various analysis to compare the impact of media preference or media types on the posttest scores. In addition, an online questionnaire (assigned to all the participants) and a semi-structured interview (only 10 participants from each of the six groups, namely 60 participants in total, were interviewed due to time and cost issues) were also employed in the study to elicit the participants' perceptions toward the learning process. The results of the posttest, the questionnaire, and the semi-structured interview are discussed in Section 5 of this paper.

...

Summarized answers from the 10 participants from Group Auditory-

Audio-only

分析：审稿人认为论文的方法部分(Method)中的实验工具(Instruments)一节似乎和内容不太相符。在其看来，作者在这一部分只描述了用于教学实验的学习材料和六种不同的实验条件，所以该审稿人建议将这一部分的小标题可以命名为"实验条件"(Experimental Conditions)或"实验小组"(Experimental Groups)。同时，审稿人还建议增加一个"学习内容"(Learning Content)小节和一个采纳"数据来源"(Data Sources)小节。审稿人还指出文章应补充有关后测(Posttest)的信息。此外，审稿人认为针对学习者对学习媒体感知的问卷和针对10名参与者的半结构访谈的相关信息也不足，希望作者补充。在回复中，作者采纳了审稿人的建议，在修改稿中将"Instruments"小节的标题改成了"Learning Content"，并增加了一个名叫"Data Sources"的小节，在这一小节详细介绍了前测、后测、问卷和访谈的相关信息。

8) Results: It would be better to structure the results according to the three research questions, meaning that 5.1. Results of the experiment should be Results of research question 1 differences in learning outcomes, the second research question has no individual heading, so that this must be completed with 5.2. Results of research question 2 influence of mismatch… and 5.3 Results of research question 3, learners' perceptions.

My response: Thanks! I have revised this part accordingly. For example:

5.2 *Results of research question 2 "influence of mismatch between media preference and received media"*

Among the 6 groups described in the present study, the complete mismatch between media preference and received media was produced in two groups, namely Group Auditory-Text-only (where auditory learners were assigned visual-only materials), and Group Visual-Audio-only (where visual learners were given audio-only materials). The complete match between media preference and received media was found in Group Auditory-Audio-only, and Group Visual-text-only. As for Group Auditory-Combined, and Group Visual-Combined, these two groups can be taken as undergoing a mixed match manipulation (in which both the preferred media type and the disfavored media type were shown). As indicated in Table 3 and Table 7, the 6 groups are in the following order from the best to the worst as far as the posttest scores are concerned: Group Visual-Combined (mixed match), Group Auditory-Combined (mixed match), Group Visual-Text-only (complete match), Group Auditory-Text-only (complete mismatch), Group Visual-Audio-only (complete mismatch), and Group

Auditory-Audio-only (complete match). From this order of learning performance, we can see that the mismatch between media preference and received media did not produce the worst result, nor the best result as well.

分析：审稿人认为实验结果(Results)部分应和前文提出的三个研究问题对应着来写(这种研究结果和研究问题一一对应的写法在本书的第二章中已做过说明)。这种意见其实是和个人的写作喜好有关,因为很多论文的实验结论部分是综合性的表述,并没有按照研究问题分开来写。但是,审稿人的合理意见我们只能接受。在回复中,我们可以看到作者完全接受了这一意见,并对实验结果部分做了结构调整,将内容和前文的研究问题一一对应了。

9) The questionnaire should be explained in the method section under "data sources" and not in the results section. Furthermore, the semi-structured interview should also be firstly explained in the method section, not in the results section.

My response：Thanks! As indicated in my previous response, I have added a new subsection named "Data Sources" in Section 4, in which the questionnaire and the semi-structured interview are introduced

分析：审稿人认为本文实验中使用的问卷和半结构访谈的相关背景信息不应放在实验结果部分来介绍,而应移至实验方法部分。作者完全接受并进行了修改。

10) I am not sure, how the semi-structured interview data should be presented. At the moment, the first question is presented very detailed, while the second question not. Eventually, the detailed answers of research question 1 could be taken into the Appendix and only the summary should be presented in the main text like in research question 2. But then, I would also present the detailed answers of research question 2 in the Appendix.

My response：Thanks! I have made some changes according to your comment. I have summarized answers to question 1 in the main text, and moved the detailed answers to question 1 to the end of the paper as Appendix B. But I still do not provide detailed answers to question 2, because the answers to question 2 from the 6 groups overlap to each other to a great extent. That's why I think there is no need for me to provide such information, and I have stated this reason in the manuscript.

分析：审稿人对于半结构访谈的结果呈现方式提出了疑问,建议将具体的访谈内容移至文末作为附录,而将访谈内容进行归纳后放在正文部分。作者在回信中接受了这一意见并进行了相应的修改。

11) Discussion: The explanations of the results are in a first step

comprehensible. But in a second step regarding Mayer's studies, this is not totally correct. Mayer's studies say that presenting information with two different channels is helpful, when the information is not redundant, but which is the case in this study. How do you explain this? The result that media preference does not affect learning outcome may be due to the fact, that there exist no specific learning styles! Please check this with the literature (Kirschner, 2017)!

My response: Thanks! I have made some clarifications in this part according to your view, but I did not mention Kirschner's study (2017) here (Kirschner's study is mentioned and discussed in previous sections), because this will bring the discussion to a much more complicated issue of "whether there is a specific learning style" raised by Kirschner (2017) and might divert readers' attention from the own topic of the present study:

This finding is consistent with Mayer's (2009) Multimedia Learning theory, in which the combination of media is more effective than a single-medium format, and presenting information with two different channels is helpful, when the information is not redundant. The possible reason why the two combined-media groups of the present study got the most successful results is that the information provided in the combined form of audio and text is not redundant but complementing and reinforcing each other. This assertion can be supported by the participants' answers to the second question of the semi-structured interview, in which all the answers indicate that the learners need the alternative media to provide them with information they might have missed in what they have already received.

分析：审稿人认为在讨论这一章，作者对于 Mayer 研究的表述不完全正确，审稿人希望作者解释一下，并认为学习者的媒体偏好没有对学习成绩产生影响的原因可能是 Kirschner（2017）文章中解释的那样。作者在回信中表示修改稿做了此方面的说明，并解释了本研究没有违反 Mayer 研究的发现，并给出了理由。但作者也明确表示，此部分不宜再次引用 Kirschner 对于学习风格是否真实存在讨论了，因为这样会使得本部分的讨论偏离文章的主题。

12) Please do not provide new results in the discussion section. You may include these in the results section. As these results belong to research question 2, they also should be mentioned there (see annotations above).

My response: Thanks! I have moved this part to subsection of 5.2.

分析：审稿人认为在文章的讨论部分不应该加入新的实验结果信息，认为此类信息应放在文章的实验结果部分。作者表示接受并做了相应修改。

13) Conclusions: The first paragraph in the conclusions is more a summary. The last sentence seems to be a conclusion. But overall, I miss a precise conclusion of the study. The second paragraph are the limitations of the study. It would be better to include limitations in the discussion section where also the strengths of the study are mentioned.

My response: Thanks! I have now added a paragraph in this section to fully state the conclusions of the present study, and the limitation paragraph has been moved to the Discussion section:

The results of the experiment on the manipulated mismatch between learning media preference and received media show that the complete mismatch will not yield the worst learning performance nor the best learning performance, and thus learners should not be curbed by their media preference when choosing learning media. In addition, the combined learning media has produced the best learning results in the present study, which may further call on learners to embrace more media types in their learning process. Moreover, the answers obtained from the questionnaire survey and the semi-structured interview imply that autonomous e-leaners need much help and assistance from teachers in the learning process with regard to the choice of learning media.

分析：审稿人认为在文章的结论这一章，第一段像是总结而非结论，第一段的最后一句似乎是个结论，但是总体来说，该审稿人认为此处缺少对整个研究的总结。而本章的第二段说的是研究局限，审稿人认为此段最好放在文章的讨论一章，因为在那一章也讨论了本研究的优点，局限和优点最好放在一起。其实，很多作者都将研究局限放在最后一章即结论部分，所以该审稿人的此条意见也属于个人写作喜好的问题，不过对于这种无关痛痒的意见，我们最好接受并作相应的修改。从作者的回信中，我们也看到作者完全接受了该条意见。

14) The originality of the paper is that it is conducted in the field with six experimental groups. I also think that there seems to be almost no studies comparing text and audio, specifically not when they are redundant. Eventually, this also could be shown as strength? But for sure, there exist a lot of studies on media presentation. I mainly wonder, whether this study is relevant, when referring to the Kirschner (2017) article. I think, the authors should refer to this article and include it when possible.

The most important point is whether this study is all in all relevant. In order to face critique regarding its relevance, the authors should include the article of Kirschner (2017). Overall, the study has some potential, specifically in a field experiment with six experimental groups. But there are also a lot of aspects which must be considered (see above).

My response：Thank you for your favorable comment on the originality of the present study, and the Kirschner (2017) article has been cited now in the paper in the Literature review section, where the citation of this article may clarify some issues related to the topic of the present study.

分析：在此条意见中，审稿人认为本研究的创新点在于在实际教学中设计了6个实验组，该审稿人认为目前很少有研究对比文本和音频这两种学习媒体，其认为或许这也算是本研究的一项优点。此外，该审稿人又一次提出作者应在文章中引用Kirschner(2017)的论文。从这名审稿人以上的意见中，可以看出他/她多次要求引用并讨论某篇文献，这种情况下，作者基本上只能接受，否则拒绝了这一条意见，与之相关的意见就不好回应了。从回信中，我们看到作者表示接受意见。

15) I have some recommendations to improve the paper: 1. Please include the paper of Kirschner (2017) in your manuscript to face possible critique. 2. Please check figures for headings and references for italics. 3. Please include data sources, experimental groups etc. in the method section (see above). 4. Please organize the results according to the research questions. 5. Please do not present new results in the discussion. 6. Please strengthen the uniqueness of the study in the beginning.

My response：Many thanks to you! Your comments are detailed and really help a lot in the revising process. I have fully considered these comments and tried my best to accommodate them in the revised version.

分析：该审稿人的最后一条意见相当于给自己前面的意见做了一个总结，其认为本文作者可以从以下几个方面来提升本文：一是引用Kirschner(2017)年的文献；二是检查插图的标题和参考文献的格式；三是在研究方法一章加入"数据来源""研究小组"等小节；四是将研究结果部分按照研究问题进行重新组织；五是在讨论部分不要加入新的研究结果；六是在文章开头突出本文的创新点。由于这是对前面所有意见的总结，而作者已经对这些意见进行了一一回复，所以此时作者再次对该审稿人表达了感谢，并表示在修改稿中已经完全考虑了这些意见并做了相关的修改。

Reviewer 3（审稿人3）：

1) I found the analysis to be competent but it was not easy to follow—probably because of the many tables. There simply was too much data for what the actual findings warranted. As a reader, I wondered how the audio and visual materials compared. Was it simply a narration (audio) of the text (visual)? That

wasn't clear.

My response: Thanks! Concerning the many tables, I have now deleted the original Table 4 (Tests of between-subjects effects), since the description of this test in the manuscript is enough for readers' understanding. Besides, the original Table 8 is moved to the end of the paper as Appendix B. As for the comparison between audio and visual materials, I have now added a paragraph to tackle this issue in the section of Literature review, and some information about the combination of the two media is also added in the section of Discussion:

The possible reason why the two combined-media groups of the present study got the most successful results is that the information provided in the combined form of audio and text is not redundant but complementing and reinforcing each other. This assertion can be supported by answers to the second question of the semi-structured interview, in which all the answers indicate that the learners need the alternative media to provide them with information they might have missed in what they have already received.

In addition, the audio materials and text materials used in the experiment are what you said in the comment: audio is the narration of the text. Actually, the two types of learning materials have been explained in the paper, and I don't know whether the confusion is caused by the wording:

Audios were recordings of the reading of the on-screen text by the instructor, namely the instructor's narration of the text.

分析：审稿人认为文章的分析虽然有效，但是不宜理解，或许是因为文中用了很多表格，显得数据过多了。该审稿人想知道听觉和视觉这两种学习材料在实验中是如何进行比较的，难道文中所说的听觉材料仅仅是对文本（视觉材料）的复述吗？文中并没有清晰说明此点。在回信中，作者针对表格过多的问题，表示在修改稿中删除了 Table 4，因为此表格的信息可以在正文中体现，Table 8 则被移到了文末作为附录。修改稿还在文献回顾部分增加了一段文字来比较视、听学习材料，同时还在文章的讨论这一章增加了有关视、听结合材料的探讨。

2) It would also be important to know how much time students in the various groups spent on the materials. For example, did the combined group spend as much time as the audio and visual groups added together?

My response: Thanks for this comment! My dear reviewer, I quite understand that if such information you mentioned here had been provided, the arguments made by the paper would have been much stronger. However, as I have stated in the subsection of 4.4 "procedure" that the learners "were given one week to study the learning materials", we can see that the learners actually were doing a one-week autonomous learning process. Hence, it was very hard to collect the exact time of every learner spent on using the learning materials during the one week. Besides, for an autonomous learning process, learners surely will differ in their learning time. In this sense, it doesn't mean much even if they spent different time in learning, so long as all of them did the learning autonomously. The overall experimental condition (all the 6 groups did autonomous learning) is the same for all the 6 groups, which will guarantee the soundness of the paper. Thank you again and I am sorry for the missing of such information.

分析：审稿人认为文章有必要写明每个组里的学生到底用了多少时间使用这些学习材料，例如，混合型学习媒体的小组花费的学习时间是否是听觉小组和视觉小组学习时间的总和呢？作者在回信中有理有据地驳斥了这一要求。作者表明，在实验方法一章的实验步骤（Procedure）一节中，我们可以看出这些小组都在进行自主学习（autonomous learning），所以每个小组里的成员到底花费多少时间来学习这些不同的媒体材料是无法确切得知的，而且不同的成员花费的自主学习时间一般也是不同的。但是，由于6个小组都在进行这样的自主学习，所以总的实验条件对于这6个小组都是一致的。也就是说，即使小组里的成员花费的学习时间不同，这也不会影响整个实验的有效性。当然，作者也表示对于此类信息的缺失感到抱歉。

3) I don't think this study as presented in the current manuscript provides the information for instructors the author(s) hoped it would. Perhaps it can be reworked if the data on time on task, etc. exists. If so, a re-submission might be warranted. However, at this point, I lean toward rejection and urge the authors to continue this research to answer more significant questions than were dealt with in this study.

My response：Many thanks to you for your hard work in reviewing my paper. If I understand this comment correctly, your decision of rejecting my paper is based on the missing of data on time spent on task. I have explained this in the previous response to your comment.

分析：该名审稿人最后一条意见表明了要拒稿，原因就在于前一条意见中提出的"学习任务的时间没有给出相关数据"，他/她认为目前的稿件无法达成该文声称的目标，但是如果作者能补充相关数据，允许稿件重投（Resubmission）。作者在回复中感谢了该名审稿人的审稿，并表明该审稿人的拒稿应该就是基于学习时间数据的缺少而做出的，作者表明对于这些数据缺失的原因在上一条意见的回复中已经说明了。其实,从我们对上一条意见的分析来看,该名审稿人的拒稿理由并不合理,因为他/她要求的这些数据对于自主学习来说很难——收集,即使进行收集,数据的准确度也很难保证。但是就实验设计来说,由于 6 个小组都是进行这种自主学习,所以大体来说这类数据的缺失并不会影响整个实验的有效性。

从三名审稿人的意见来看,有两位审稿人倾向于拒稿(审稿人 1 和审稿人 3),但是编辑并没有拒稿,可见编辑还是比较喜欢本论文探讨的话题的。由于在第一次应答信中,作者对于这些不利的审稿意见进行了解释、驳斥,且有理有据,所以编辑又进行了二次送审。我们来看看二次送审后返回的审稿意见。

Reviewer 1(审稿人 1):

The manuscript was very much improved. Great work! I put my annotations directly into the manuscript. There are only some few issues, I would improve before publication. It's not very much work any more.

My response: Thank you, my dear reviewer! I have read your annotations and done the revision based on them, and all the revisions are marked in purple. In particular, I have checked the references and make sure that all literature mentioned in the text is part of the reference section.

分析: 审稿人认为修改稿有了很大的提升,并在原文中对应该修改的地方做了批注,让作者根据这次的批注再做修改,而且这些修改之处都是一些小问题,工作量不大。作者在回信中表示了感谢,并再次根据意见进行了修改。

Reviewer 2(审稿人 2):

Comments to the Author

The revised manuscript is a definite improvement on the original. The added qualifications of the Learning Style concept was needed and the author provided a thoughtful discussion of that. The post test data validated the discussion in that no differences were found for learning style. However, two problems remain. The first is stylistic—there remains too much outside the text of the article. Tables and appendices or whatever the author calls them provide information that could simply be noted in the text. This is not an insurmountable problem but the second one, in my opinion, is more serious. In a reply to the time on task issue raised in my earlier review, the author said it was not possible to obtain this data. It certainly is not easy data to obtain but the simple alternative explanation to the important combined media advantage is that students spent more time on the learning task because they had two modes of input (audio + visual) to process instead of one (audio or visual) leading to more time on task—an obvious factor in learning. The paper is clearer and more circumspect overall but also clearer is that there isn't a great deal the author can say about the results. I urge the author to continue to refine the methods that I expect will lead to more significant understanding of this type of learning environment.

My response：Thank you, dear reviewer! I have made some revisions according to your comments. In particular, I have accommodated your comment on the time on task issue in the Discussion section as one of the explanation to why the combined media assignment has advantages over the other two media assignment forms：

An alternative explanation to the important combined media advantage is that students spent more time on the learning task because they had two modes of input (audio plus visual) to process instead of one (audio or visual). In other words, the processing of the two modes of input will lead to more time spent on task, which is an obvious factor for improving learning performance.

分析：这位审稿人应该就是上次做了拒稿决定的审稿人3，不过这一次该审稿人并没有坚持再次拒稿了。他/她也认为作者的修改稿有了很大提升，不过对于上次提出的学习时间数据的问题，该审稿人还是认为即使作者无法收集到这类信息，也应该在讨论部分提及可能正是由于学生利用综合媒体类学习资源的学习时间长于利用单一媒体学习资源的学习时间，才使得利用综合媒体资源进行学习的学生取得了更好的学习效果。作者在回信中表示，二次修改时在论文的讨论部分采纳了这一意见，并进行了补充。

从上面两个真实案例中可以看出，当编辑给作者大修机会时，作者对于修改意见一定要尽可能地满足；而对于审稿人偏颇或错误的意见，要有理有据地进行有礼貌的反驳，语言要尽量委婉。

3.4 接收后事项

无论大修还是小修，只要作者进行了认真修改，论文被接收的可能性是很大的。此时，最让人兴奋的莫过于收到编辑发来的接收函了。在接收函中，编辑会提醒作者后续会有期刊的出版部门（Production Team）发来要求校对论文清样（Proof）的邮件，以及要求填写一些版权转移表格、是否开源（Open Access）、纸质版论文是否要求彩色、是否订购纸质版论文（Offprint）的邮件。一般来说，除非我们有资金支持或者真正有需要，否则作者在填这些表格时，选择免费的选项即可。

需要注意的是，在校对清样时，一定要看清楚作者姓名、单位、资助基金等信息,因为论文发表前只有一次校对清样的机会,当作者在线提交了清样后,就没有机会修改论文内容和这些重要信息了。图 3-6 所示为一个 Elsevier 出品期刊的在线校样系统,该系统很成熟,首页上会给作者一系列详细的说明。有的期刊对于接收的论文在线出版的速度非常快。就拿笔者曾经发表的一篇论文来说,该期刊是 Elsevier 出品,论文被接收后的第三天就已经可以在该期刊的网站看到这篇论文的在线版本了。图 3-7 所示为 Taylor & Francis 出版社的在线校稿系统,该系统也是非常成熟、好用,可以让作者在线回复编辑在校稿环节对文章提出的疑问,也允许作者在线对文章进行相应的修改。

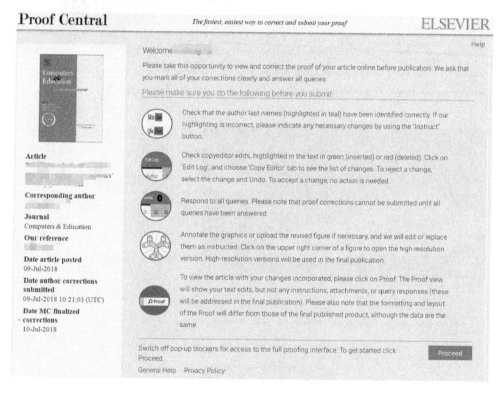

图 3-6　Elsevier 的在线校稿系统

当作者校稿完毕并提交后,这篇论文从写作到发表的整个过程也即将画上句号。此后,经过一定的时间(一般时间都很短),论文的网络优先版本(online first)就会出现在期刊的网站上。再过一段时间,在 SSCI 数据库就可以检索到发表的论文了。对于这篇论文来说,它的 SSCI 发表之路算是到达了终点。

图 3-7 Taylor & Francis 在线校稿系统

参 考 文 献

[1] Al-Rahmi W. M., Alias N., Othman M. S., et al. A model of factors affecting learning performance through the use of social media in Malaysian higher education[J]. Computers & Education, 2018, 121:59-72.

[2] Bahreini K., Nadolski R., Westera, W. Communication skills training exploiting multimodal emotion recognition [J]. Interactive Learning Environments, 2017, 25(8):1065-1082.

[3] Bano M., Zowghi D., Kearney M., et al. Mobile learning for science and mathematics school education: A systematic review of empirical evidence [J]. Computers & Education, 2018, 121:30-58.

[4] Barak M. Are digital natives open to change? Examining flexible thinking and resistance to change [J]. Computers & Education, 2018, 121:115-123.

[5] Barak M., Asakle S. AugmentedWorld: Facilitating the creation of location-based questions[J]. Computers & Education, 2018, 121:89-99.

[6] Brown C., Spiro H., Quinton, S. The role of research ethics committees: Friend or foe in educational research? An exploratory study[J]. British Educational Research Journal, 2020, 46(4):747-769.

[7] Choi M., Cristol D., Gimbert, B. Teachers as digital citizens: The influence of individual backgrounds, internet use and psychological characteristics on teachers' levels of digital citizenship[J]. Computers & Education, 2018, 121:143-161.

[8] Chou P. N., Chang C. C., Chen M. Y. Let's Draw: Utilizing Interactive

White Board to Support Kindergarten Children's Visual Art Learning Practice[J]. Educational Technology & Society, 2017, 20(4):89-101.

[9] Claro M., Salinas A., Cabello-Hutt T., et al. Teaching in a Digital Environment (TIDE): Defining and measuring teachers' capacity to develop students' digital information and communication skills [J]. Computers & Education, 2018, 121:162-174.

[10] Cordewener K. A. H., Hasselman F., Verhoeven L., et al. The Role of Instruction for Spelling Performance and Spelling Consciousness[J]. The Journal of Experimental Education, 2018, 86(2):135-153.

[11] Dowling P. Whiteman, N. Authority and ethics: A case for estrangement in educational research and research education[J]. British Educational Research Journal, 2020, 46(4):770-785.

[12] Durand R., Hawn O, Ioannou, I. Willing and able: A general model of organizational responses to normative pressures [J]. Academy of Management Review, 2019, 44(2): 299-320.

[13] Fisher G. Online communities and firm advantages. Academy of Management Review 2019, 44(2):279-298.

[14] Förster M., Weiser C., Maur, A. How feedback provided by voluntary electronic quizzes affects learning outcomes of university students in large classes[J]. Computers & Education, 2018, 121:100-114.

[15] Ge Z. G. Exploring e-learners' perceptions of net-based peer-reviewed English writing [J]. International Journal of Computer-Supported Collaborative Learning, 2011, 6(1):75-91.

[16] Ge Z. G. Enhancing Vocabulary Retention by Embedding L2 Target Words in L1 Stories: An Experiment with Chinese Adult e-Learners[J]. Journal of Educational Technology & Society, 2015, 18(3):254-265.

[17] Ge Z. G. The impact of a forfeit-or-prize gamified teaching on e-learners' learning performance[J]. Computers & Education, 2018, 126:143-152.

[18] Ge Z. G. Does mismatch between learning media preference and received learning media bring a negative impact on Academic performance? An experiment with e-learners[J]. Interactive Learning Environments, 2019,

DOI：10.1080/10494820.2019.1612449.

[19] Gill M. J. The significance of suffering in organizations: Understanding variation in workers' responses to multiple modes of control[J]. Academy of Management Review, 2019, 44(2):377-404.

[20] Gleason N. Sprankle, E. The effects of pornography on sexual minority men's body image: an experimental study[J]. Psychology & Sexuality, 10(4):301-315.

[21] Glynn M. A. 2018 Presidential address—the mission of community and the promise of collective action[J]. Academy of Management Review, 2019, 44(2):244-253.

[22] Hamari J., Keronen, L. Why do peoplebuy virtual goods: A meta-analysis[J]. Computers in Human Behavior, 2017, 71:59-69.

[23] Herodotou C. Mobile games and science learning: A comparative study of 4 and 5 years old playing the game Angry Birds[J]. British Journal of Educational Technology, 2018, 49(1): 6-16.

[24] Hsu C. C., Wang T. I. Applying game mechanics and student-generated questions to an online puzzle-based game learning system to promote algorithmic thinking skills[J]. Computers & Education, 2018, 121:73-88.

[25] Huisman B., Admiraal W., Pilli O., et al. Peer assessment in MOOCs: The relationship between peer reviewers' ability and authors' essay performance[J]. British Journal of Educational Technology, 2018, 49(1):101-110.

[26] Huisman B., Saab N., van Driel J., et al. Peer feedback on academic writing: undergraduate students' peer feedback role, peer feedback perceptions and essay performance[J]. Assessment & Evaluation in Higher Education, 2018, 43(6):955-968.

[27] Hylton K., Levy Y., Dringus, L. P. Utilizing webcam-based proctoring to deter misconduct in online exams[J]. Computers & Education, 2016, 92-93:53-63.

[28] Hummel H. G. K., Boyle E. A., Einarsdóttir S., et al. Game-based

career learning support for youth: effects of playing the Youth@Work game on career adaptability[J]. Interactive Learning Environments, 2018, 26(6):745-759.

[29] Kirschner P. Stop propagating the learning styles myth[J]. Computers & Education, 2017, 106:166-171.

[30] Kordaki M., Gousiou A. Computer Card Games in Computer Science Education[J]. Journal of Educational Technology & Society, 2016, 19(4):11-21.

[31] Kudesia R. S. Mindfulness as metacognitive practice[J]. Academy of Management Review, 2019, 44(2):405-423.

[32] Lee Y. H. Scripting to enhance university students' critical thinking in flipped learning: implications of the delayed effect on science reading literacy[J]. Interactive Learning Environments, 2017, (5):1-14.

[33] Lee J. Bonk, C. J. (2016). Social networkanalysis of peer relationships and online interactions in a blended class using blogs[J]. Internet & Higher Education, 2016, 28:35-44.

[34] Li X., McAllister D. J., Ilies R., et al. Schadenfreude: A counternormative observer response to workplace mistreatment. Academy of Management Review [J], 2019, 44(2):360-376.

[35] Liew T. W., Tan S. M. The Effects of Positive and Negative Mood on Cognition and Motivation in Multimedia Learning Environment[J]. Journal of Educational Technology & Society, 2016, 19(2):104-115.

[36] Lin G. Y. Anonymous versus identified peer assessment via a Facebook-based learning application: Effects on quality of peer feedback, perceived learning, perceived fairness, and attitude toward the system[J]. Computers & Education, 2018, 116:81-92.

[37] Lin Y. R., Fan, B., Xie, K. The influence of a web-based learning environment on low achievers' science argumentation[J/OL]. Computers & Education, 2020, 151. Retrieved from https://www.sciencedirect.com/science/article/pii/S0360131520300609.

[38] Lye S. Y., Koh J. H. L. Review on teaching and learning of computational

thinking through programming: what is next for k-12? [J]. Computers in Human Behavior, 2014, 41: 51-61.

[39] Mathrani A., Christian S., Ponder-Sutton A. PlayIT: Game Based Learning Approach for Teaching Programming Concepts[J]. Journal of Educational Technology & Society, 2016, 19(2):5-17.

[40] Papadakis S., Kalogiannakis M., Zaranis N. Educational apps from the Android Google Play for Greek preschoolers: A systematic review[J]. Computers & Education, 2018, 116:139-160.

[41] Parker O., Krause R., Devers C. E. How firm reputation shapes managerial discretion[J]. Academy of Management Review, 2019, 44(2): 254-278.

[42] Puranik H., Koopman J., Vough H. C., et al. They want what I've got (I think): The causes and consequences of attributing coworker behavior to envy[J]. Academy of Management Review, 2019, 44(2):424-449.

[43] Qian M., Clark K. R. Game-based Learning and 21st century skills: A review of recent research[J]. Computers in Human Behavior, 2016, 63: 50-58.

[44] Sadowski A. S., Lomanowska A. M. Virtual intimacy: Propensity for physical contact between avatars in an online virtual environment[J]. Computers in Human Behavior, 2018, 78:1-9.

[45] Sun Z., Xie K., Anderman, L. H. The role of self-regulated learning in students' success in flipped undergraduate math courses[J]. The Internet and Higher Education,2018, 36: 41-53.

[46] Tsai Y. h., Lin C. h., Hong J. c., et al. The effects of metacognition on online learning interest and continuance to learn with MOOCs[J]. Computers & Education, 2018,121:18-29.

[47] Tsay C. H. H., Kofinas A., Luo J. Enhancing student learning experience with technology-mediated gamification: An empirical study[J]. Computers & Education, 2018, 121:1-17.

[48] Tu M., Cheng Z., Liu W. Spotlight on the effect of workplace ostracism on creativity: a social cognitive perspective [J/OL]. Frontiers in

Psychology, 2019, 10. Retrieved from https://www.frontiersin.org/articles/10.3389/fpsyg.2019.01215/full.

[49] Van Ginkel S., Gulikers J., Biemans H., et al. Fostering oral presentation performance: does the quality of feedback differ when provided by the teacher, peers or peers guided by tutor?[J]. Assessment & Evaluation in Higher Education, 2017, 42(6): 953-966.

[50] Vega-Hernández M. C., Patino-Alonso M. C., Galindo-Villardón M. P. Multivariate characterization of university students using the ICT for learning[J]. Computers & Education, 2018, 121: 124-130.

[51] Waeger D., Weber K. Institutional complexity and organizational change: An open polity perspective[J]. Academy of Management Review, 2019, 44(2): 336-359.

[52] Wang F. H. An exploration of online behaviour engagement and achievement in flipped classroom supported by learning management system[J]. Computers & Education, 2017, 114: 79-91.

[53] Wang S., Zhang K., Du M., et al. Development and measurement validity of an instrument for the impact of technology-mediated learning on learning processes[J]. Computers & Education, 2018, 121: 131-142.

[54] Weik E. Understanding institutional endurance: The role of dynamic form, harmony, and rhythm in institutions[J]. Academy of Management Review, 2019, 44(2): 321-335.